# A Beginners Guide for OOPS Concepts in Java Programming

Dr.R. Anandan, B.E., M.S., Ph.D.,

Chartered Engineer, Professor,

Department of Computer Science and Engineering,

School of Engineering, Vels Institute of Science,

Technology and Advanced Studies (VISTAS),

Pallavaram, Chennai - 117.

Sreenivasulu Bolla, B.Tech., M.Tech.

Assistant Professor, Department of CSE,

PACE Institute of Technology and Sciences,

ONGOLE- 523 272, Prakasam District, Andhra Pradesh.

Sindhe Phani Kumar, M.Tech,

Assistant Professor, Department of CSE,

PACE Institute of Technology and Sciences,

ONGOLE- 523 272 Prakasam District, Andhra Pradesh.

Published by

BONFRING®
Intellectual Integrity

AF528403

**A Beginners Guide for OOPS Concepts in Java Programming**



9 789387 862449 >

**ISBN 978-93-87862-44-9**

**Authors**

Dr.R. Anandan

Sreenivasulu Bolla

Sindhe Phani Kumar

**Bonfring**

309, 2nd Floor,

5th Street Extension, Gandhipuram,

Coimbatore-641 012.

Tamilnadu, India.

E-mail: info@bonfring.org

Website: www.bonfring.org

Phone: 0422 4213231

# Preface

The book **"A Beginners Guide For OOPS Concepts in Java Programming"** is the consequence of our remarkable work. It is the versatile work that every Engineering and Computer Science students to posses. **Dr.R. Anandan**, Professor, Department of CSE, School of Engineering, VELS Institute of Science, Technology and Advanced Studies (VISTAS),Pallavaram, Chennai – 117, **Mr. Sreenivasulu Bolla,** Department of CSE, PACE Institute of Technology and Sciences, Research Scholar VISTAS and **Mr.S. Phani Kumar**, Department of CSE. PACE Institute of Technology and Sciences, Research Scholar VISTAS. The idea of publishing the book **" A Beginners Guide for OOPS Concepts in Java Programming"** dawned in our minds which would be of great benefit to Engineering and Computer Science students.

**A Beginners Guide for OOPS Concepts in Java Programming** is one of the most significant areas of Computer Science that has its applications in almost every field. This book **A Beginners Guide for OOPS Concepts in Java Programming** has been authored to help students to learn basic concepts and techniques in with ease.

This book has been prepared as per the syllabus of most of the Indian Foreign Universities and for the courses B.E./B.Sc/BCA/M.Sc./MCA.

All the units are explained vividly in a lucid manner. An attempt has been made to keep the language as simple as possible and students will definitely be able to appreciate thisbook.

We hope that this book will be of great help for the students to understand the subject which in turn will help them to do well in their examination.

Suggestions for further improvement of the book will be thankfully acknowledged.

***Dr.R. Anandan***
***Sreenivasulu Bolla***
***Sindhe Phani Kumar***

# Acknowledgement

We owe our heartfelt gratitude to respected Chancellor of Vels Institute of Science, Technology and Advance Studies (VISTAS) **Dr. Ishari K. Ganesh, M.Com., M.B.A., B.L., Ph.D.,** and **Dr. Aarthi Ganesh.,** Pro-Chancellor (Academic) for providing us with an opportunity to author this book.

A deep sense of gratitude to **Dr.A. Jothi Murugan,** Vice President (Planning and Development) of Vels Institute of Science, Technology and Advance Studies (VISTAS) for his rock solid backing and unstinted support he has given throughout this long and ardours travail.

Our sincere thanks to **Dr.P. Swaminathan**, Vice Chancellor for motivating us to move on into the path of innovation and research and publication of books.

We wish to place on record our gratitude to **Dr.A.R. Veeramani**, Registrar for being a source of encouragement to this great endeavor of ours.

We express our gratitude to **Dr.E.N. Ganesh**, Dean, School of Engineering, **Mrs.K. Kalaivani**, Head, Department of CSE, School of Engineering for their support and guidance.

We would like to thank to **Dr.M. Venu Gopal Rao**, Chairman and **Dr.M. Sridhar**, Secretary & Correspondent, PACE Institute of Technology & Sciences for giving me an opportunity to reach my goal.

We would like to extend special thanks to the Principal **Dr.M. Sreenivasan**, PACE Institute of Technology & Sciences, who encouraged me to complete my task.

We would like to thank **Dr.T.R. Chaitanya**, HOD of CSE, PACE Institute of Technology & Sciences, extended valuable support that goes a long way for my academic progress.

We take this opportunity to thank our colleagues for their support and assistance. We thank profusely all those who have helped us in some way or other in bringing out this book

We thank the publisher for his painstaking effort in bringing out this book. Any suggestion for the improvement of the book is most welcome.

***Dr.R. Anandan***

***Sreenivasulu Bolla***

***Sindhe Phani Kumar***

# Authors Profile

**Dr.R. Anandan** received his Under Graduate in Computer Science and Engineering from University of Madras Masters from Birla Institute of Technology and Science. Pilani and Doctoral degree in Computer Science and Engineering from BIHER, Chennai.

He is IBMS/390 Mainframe professional and he is recognized as Chartered Engineer from Institution of Engineers in India and received fellowship from Bose Science Society, India.

He is currently working as Professor, Department of Computing Science and Engineering, School of Engineering, Vels Institute of Science, Technology & Advanced Studies (VISTAS), Chennai, Tamil Nadu, India which is Pioneer Institution in Engineering. He has vast experience in corporate and all levels of Academic in Computer Science and Engineering his knowledge of interests not limited to Artificial intelligence Soft Computing, Machine Learning, High Performance Computing, Bigdata Analytics, Image Processing,3D printing and knowledge Engineering. Under his eminent guidance 8Ph.D Research Scholars are pursuing, under his Supervision.

He associated as Member in many reputed International and National societies like International Association of Engineers (IAENG) Hong Kong, Computer Science Teacher Association (CSTA) New York, Universal Association of Computer and Electronics Engineers, USA, Association of Computer Sciences and Information Technology (IACSIT), Singapore, Institution of Engineers, India, Computer Society of India and Indian Society of Technical Education (I.S.T.E).

He serves as Editorial Board Member / Technical Committee/ Reviewer of International Journal such Arab/UK/USA journals (Springer, Thomson Reuter).

He servers as International Committee Members towards International Conference conducted in association with Springer and Scopus.

He has published more than 80 research papers in various International Journals indexed in Scopus, SCI and referred journal. He received best reviewer award for the year 2017- 2018 from International Arab Journal of Information Technology (SCI Journal) under Elsevier Publication, Netherland and the reviewer of the year 2018 - 2019 from Energy Review Elsevier Publication, Amsterdam, Netherland. He received Appreciation award on Teachers Day towards publication of articles for the academic year 2017-2018. He is the Recipient of the awards Dr APJ ABDUL KALAM BEST SCIENTIST AWARD for Computer Science Engineering from BOSE Science Society, Tamil Nadu, India ,Distinguished Researcher in Artificial Intelligence Award by Research under Literal Access Awards, India, Outstanding Scientist award by International Research Awards on Engineering, Science and Management, Award for excellence in Young Researcher in Computer Science Engineering by Global Outreach Research, New Delhi, India and Distinguished Professor from Vedant Academics Bangkok Awards – 2019 at Kasetsart University, Chatuchak, Bangkok, Thailand

He filed two Patents of his Research works. He authored books in Software Engineering, Big data and Hadoop, Functions of Hardware and Internet, Advanced Java Programming and Chapters in leading publications.

**Sreenivasulu Bolla** received his B.Tech Degree in Computer Science & Engineering from J.N.T.U Kakinada, in the year 2011.Did his M.Tech Degree in Computer Science & Engineering from J.N.T.U Kakinada, in the year 2014. Presently pursuing Ph.Din the area of **"Big Data Analytics"** in the Department of Computer Science& Engineering from VELS Institute of Science, Technology & Advanced Studies, Chennai. He has 6 years of Teaching Experience. He has published 5 papers in various National & International journals. He has attended 8 seminars and workshops. He got number of NPTEL online course certificates from IIT Madras .He is currently working as an Assistant Professor in the Department of Computer Science & Engineering, PACE Institute of Technology & Sciences, Ongole, Prakasam District, Andhra Pradesh.

**Sindhe Phani Kumar** is a research scholar in the department of CSE, VELS Institute of Science, Technology & Advanced Studies. He completed his Masters in Web Technologies from JNTUH in 2012. He is currently working as Assistant Professor in the department of CSE, PACE Institute of Technology & Sciences. He developed many applications for educational institutions and he received Outstanding Faculty award in 2018. His research interests Big Data Analytics, Cloud Computing and Web Technologies.

# CHAPTER I

## Introduction to OOP

### 1.1. Introduction to OOP

- **Object-oriented programming** (OOP) is a programming Paradigm based on the concept of "objects", which are data structures that contain data, in the form of fields, often known as *attributes;* and code, in the form of procedures, often known as *methods.*
- A distinguishing feature of objects is that an object's procedures can access and often modify the data fields of the object with which they are associated (objects have a notion of "this").
- In object-oriented programming, computer programs are designed by making them out of objects that interact with one another. There is significant diversity in object-oriented programming, but most popular languages are class-based, meaning that objects are instances of classes, which typically also determines their type.
- Many of the most widely used programming languages are multi-paradigm
- Programming Languages that support object-oriented programming to a greater or lesser degree, typically in combination with imperative, procedural programming.
- Significant object-oriented languages include C++, Objective-C, Smalltalk, Delphi, Java, C#, Perl, Python, Ruby and PHP.
- Objects sometimes correspond to things found in the real world. For example, a graphics program may have objects such as "circle," "square," "menu."
- An online shopping system will have objects such as "shopping cart," "customer," and "product." The shopping system will support behaviors such as "place order," "make payment," and "offer discount."
- Objects are designed in class hierarchies. For example, with the shopping system there might be high level classes such as "electronics product," "kitchen product," and "book."
- There may be further refinements for example under "electronic products": "CD Player," "DVD player," etc.

## 1.2. Need of OOP

- When we are going to work with classes and objects we always think why there is need of classes and object although without classes and objects our code works well. But after some work on classes and objects we think, it's better to work with classes and objects.
- And then we can understand that Object oriented Programming is better than procedural Programming. Object oriented programming requires a different way of thinking about how can we construct our application.
- **Let's take a short example:**

When we are going to build a house .We distribute the works needed to make a house we can divide the works in different part and deliver to different persons like plumber for water supply, electrician for electricity etc. The electrician doesn't need to know that the work of plumber and vice versa.

In the same way in Object Oriented Programming we can divide our applications in different modules called classes. And one class is separate from other classes .It has its own functionality and features.

- So what advantages we can get from Object Oriented Programming:
  1. **Reusability Of Code**: In object oriented programming one class can easily copied to another application if we want to use its functionality, **EX:** When we work with hospital application and railway reservation application .In both application we need person class so we have to write only one time the person class and it can easily use in other application.
  2. **Easily Discover a bug**: When we work with procedural programming it take a lot of time to discover a bug and resolve it .But in object Oriented Programming due to modularity of classes we can easily discover the bug and we have to change in one class only and this change make in all the application only by changing it one class only.

## 1.3. Principles of Object Oriented Languages

The Objects Oriented Programming (OOP) is constructed over four major principles:

1. Encapsulation,
2. Data Abstraction,
3. Polymorphism
4. Inheritance.

### *1. Encapsulation*

Encapsulation means that the internal representation of an object is generally hidden from view outside of the object's definition.

Typically, only the object's own methods can directly inspect or manipulate its fields. Encapsulation is the hiding of data implementation by restricting access to **accessors** and **mutators**.

An **accessor** is a method that is used to ask an object about itself. In OOP, these are usually in the form of properties, which have a ***get*** method, which is an accessor method. However, accessor methods are not restricted to properties and can be any public method that gives information about the state of the object.

A **Mutator** is public method that is used to modify the state of an object, while hiding the implementation of exactly how the data gets modified. It's the ***set*** method that lets the caller modify the member data behind the scenes.

Hiding the internals of the object protects its integrity by preventing users from setting the internal data of the component into an invalid or inconsistent state. This type of data protection and implementation protection is called ***Encapsulation.*** A benefit of encapsulation is that it can reduce system complexity.

### *2. Abstraction*

Data abstraction and encapsulation are closely tied together, because a simple definition of data abstraction is the development of classes, objects, types in terms of their interfaces and functionality, instead of their implementation details. Abstraction denotes a model, a view, or some other focused representation for an actual item.

According to **Graddy Booch,** "An abstraction denotes the essential characteristics of an object that distinguish it from all other kinds of object and thus provide crisply defined conceptual boundaries, relative to the perspective of the viewer."

In short, data abstraction is nothing more than the implementation of an object that contains the same essential properties and actions we can find in the original object we are representing.

### *3. Inheritance*

Inheritance is a way to reuse code of existing objects, or to establish a subtype from an existing object, or both, depending upon programming language support.

In classical inheritance where objects are defined by classes, classes can inherit attributes and behaviour from pre-existing classes called base classes, super classes, parent classes or ancestor classes.

The resulting classes are known as derived classes, subclasses or child classes. The relationships of classes through inheritance give rise to a hierarchy.

### *4. Polymorphism*

Polymorphism means one name, many forms. Polymorphism manifests itself by having multiple methods all with the same name, but slightly different functionality.

There are 2 basic types of polymorphism. **Overriding**, also called run-time polymorphism. For method overloading, the compiler determines which method will be executed, and this decision is made when the code gets compiled.

**Overloading**, which is referred to as compile-time polymorphism. Method will be used for method overriding is determined at runtime based on the dynamic type of an object.

## 1.4. Procedural Languages Vs OOP

When programming any system you are essentially dealing with data and the code that change that data. These two fundamental aspects of programming are handled quite differently in procedural systems compared with object oriented systems, and these differences require different strategies in how we think about writing code.

### *Procedural Programming*

- In procedural programming our code is organized into small procedures that use and change our data. We write our procedures as either custom tags or functions.
- These functions typically take some input, do something, and then produce some output. Ideally your functions would behave as "black boxes" where input data goes in and output data comes out.
- The key idea here is that our functions have no intrinsic relationship with the data they operate on. As long as you provide the correct number and type of arguments, the function will do its work and faithfully return its output.
- Sometimes our functions need to access data that is not provided as a parameter, i.e., we need access data that is outside the function. Data accessed in this way is considered "global" or "shared" data.

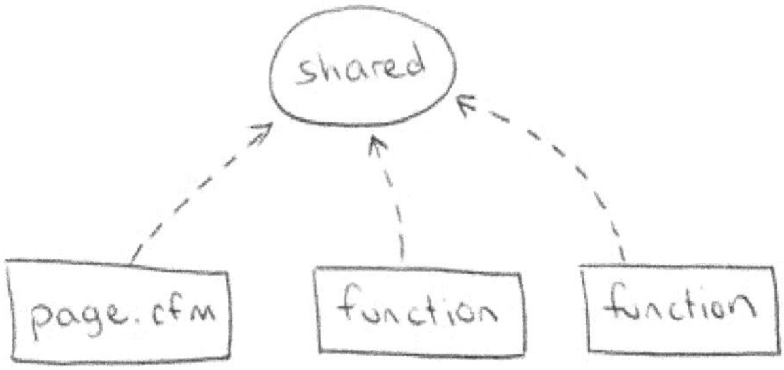


So in a procedural system our functions use data they are "given" (as parameters) but also directly access any shared data they need.

### *Object Oriented Programming*

- In object oriented programming, the data and related functions are bundled together into an "object". Ideally, the data inside an object can only be manipulated by calling the object's functions.
- This means that your data is locked away inside your objects and your functions provide the only means of doing something with that data. In a well designed object oriented system objects never access shared or global data, they are only permitted to use the data they have, or data they are given.

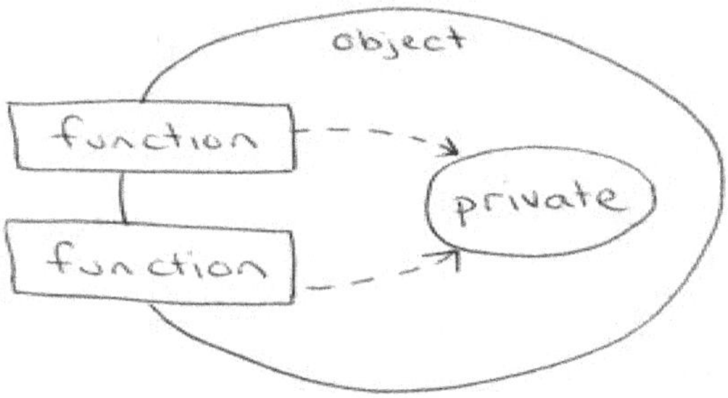


### *Global and Shared Data*

We can see that one of the principle differences is that procedural systems make use of shared and global data, while object oriented systems lock their data privately away in objects.

Let's consider a scenario where you need to change a shared variable in a procedural system. Perhaps you need to rename it, change it from a string to a numeric, change it from a struct to an array, or even remove it completely.

In a procedural application you would need to find and change each place in the code where that variable is referenced. In a large system this can be a widespread and difficult change to make.

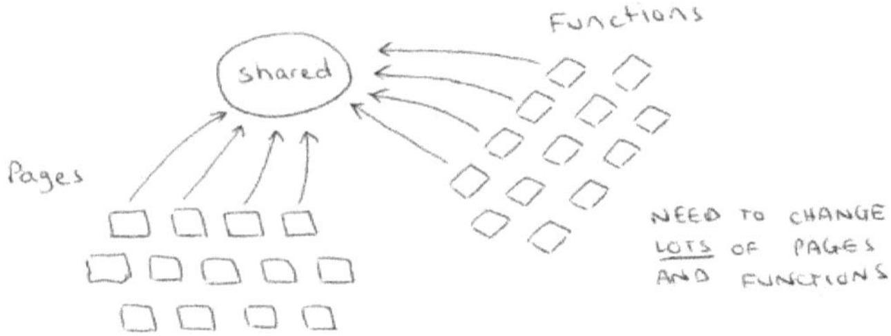


In an object oriented system we know that all variables are inside objects and that only functions within those objects can access or change those variables. When a variable needs to be changed then we only need to change the functions that access those variables.

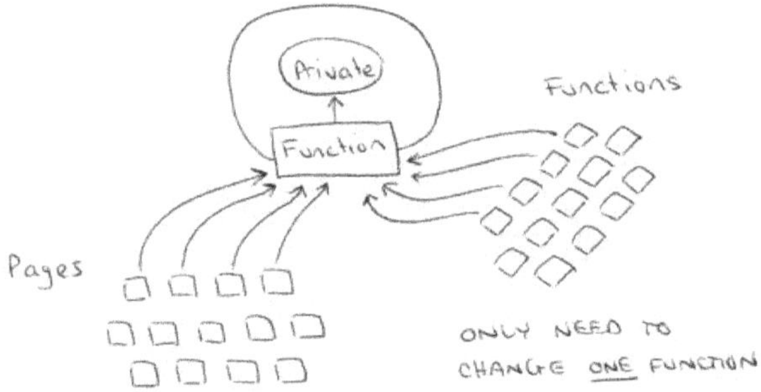


As long as we take care that the functions' input arguments and output types are not changed, then we don't need to change any other part of the system.

## 1.5. Applications of OOP

Applications of OOP are beginning to gain importance in many areas. The most important application is user interface design. Real business systems are more complex and contain many attributes and methods, but OOP applications can simplify a complex problem.

### *Application Areas*

- Computer animation
- To design Compiler
- To access relational data base
- To develop administrative tools and system tools
- Simulation and modeling
- To develop computer games

### *OOP Provides Many Applications*

**Real Time Systems:** A real time system is a system that give output at given instant and its parameters changes at every time. A real time system is nothing but a dynamic system. Dynamic means the system that changes every moment based on input to the system.

OOP approach is very useful for Real time system because code changing is very easy in OOP system and it leads toward dynamic behavior of OOP codes thus more suitable to real time System.

### *Simulation and Modeling*

System modeling is another area where criteria for OOP approach is countable. Representing a system is very easy in OOP approach because OOP codes are very easy to understand and thus is preferred to represent a system in simpler form.

### *Hypertext and Hypermedia*

Hypertext and hypermedia is another area where OOP approach is spreading its legs. Its ease of using OOP codes that makes it suitable for various media approaches.

### *Decision Support System*

Decision support system is an example of Real time system that too very advance and complex system. More details is explained in real time system

### *CAM/CAE/CAD System*

Computer has wide use of OOP approach. This is due to time saving in writing OOP codes and dynamic behavior of OOP codes.

### *Office Automation System*

Automation system is just a part or type of real time system. Embedded systems make it easy to use OOP for automated system.

### *AI And Expert System*

It is mixed system having both hypermedia and real time system.

## 1.6. History of Java

- Brief history of Java
- Java Version History

**Java history** is interesting to know. The history of java starts from Green Team. Java team members (also known as **Green Team**), initiated a revolutionary task to develop a language for digital devices such as set-top boxes, televisions etc.

For the green team members, it was an advance concept at that time. But, it was suited for internet programming. Later, Java technology as incorporated by Netscape.

**James Gosling**

Currently, Java is used in internet programming, mobile devices, games, e-business solutions etc. There are given the major points that describe the history of java.

1) **James Gosling**, **Mike Sheridan**, and **Patrick Naughton** initiated the Java language project in June 1991. The small team of sun engineers called **Green Team**.
2) Originally designed for small, embedded systems in electronic appliances like set-top boxes.
3) Firstly, it was called **"Greentalk"** by James Gosling and file extension was .gt.
4) After that, it was called **Oak** and was developed as a part of the Green project.

### *Why Oak Name for Java Language?*

5) **Why Oak?** Oak is a symbol of strength and chosen as a national tree of many countries like U.S.A., France, Germany, Romania etc.
6) In 1995, Oak was renamed as **"Java"** because it was already a trademark by Oak Technologies.

### *Why Java Name for Java Language?*

7) **Why they choose java name for java language?** The team gathered to choose a new name. The suggested words were "dynamic", "revolutionary", "Silk", "jolt", "DNA" etc. They wanted something that reflected the essence of the technology: revolutionary, dynamic, lively, cool, unique, and easy to spell and fun to say.

According to James Gosling "Java was one of the top choices along with **Silk**". Since java was so unique, most of the team members preferred java.

8) Java is an island of Indonesia where first coffee was produced (called java coffee).
9) Notice that Java is just a name not an acronym.
10) Originally developed by James Gosling at Sun Microsystems (which is now a subsidiary of Oracle Corporation) and released in 1995.
11) In 1995, Time magazine called **Java one of the Ten Best Products of 1995**.
12) JDK 1.0 released in (January 23, 1996).

### *Java Version History*

There are many java versions that have been released. Current stable release of Java is Java SE 8.

1. JDK Alpha and Beta (1995)
2. JDK 1.0 (23rd Jan, 1996)
3. JDK 1.1 (19th Feb, 1997)
4. J2SE 1.2 (8th Dec, 1998)
5. J2SE 1.3 (8th May, 2000)
6. J2SE 1.4 (6th Feb, 2002)
7. J2SE 5.0 (30th Sep, 2004)
8. Java SE 6 (11th Dec, 2006)
9. Java SE 7 (28th July, 2011)
10. Java SE 8 (18th March, 2014)

## 1.7. Java Virtual Machine

JVM (Java Virtual Machine) is an abstract machine. It is a specification that provides runtime environment in which java byte code can be executed.

JVMs are available for many hardware and software platforms (i.e. JVM is platform dependent).

### *What is JVM?*

It is:

1. **A specification** where working of Java Virtual Machine is specified. But implementation provider is independent to choose the algorithm. Its implementation has been provided by Sun and other companies.
2. **An implementation** Its implementation is known as JRE (Java Runtime Environment).
3. **Runtime Instance** Whenever you write java command on the command prompt to run the java class, and instance of JVM is created.

### *What it does?*

The JVM performs following operation:

- Loads code
- Verifies code
- Executes code
- Provides runtime environment

### *Internal Architecture of JVM*

Let's understand the internal architecture of JVM. It contains class loader, memory area, execution engine etc.

#### 1) Class loader

Class loader is a subsystem of JVM that is used to load class files.

#### 2) Class (Method) Area

Class (Method) Area stores per-class structures such as the runtime constant pool, field and method data, the code for methods.

#### 3) Heap

It is the runtime data area in which objects are allocated.

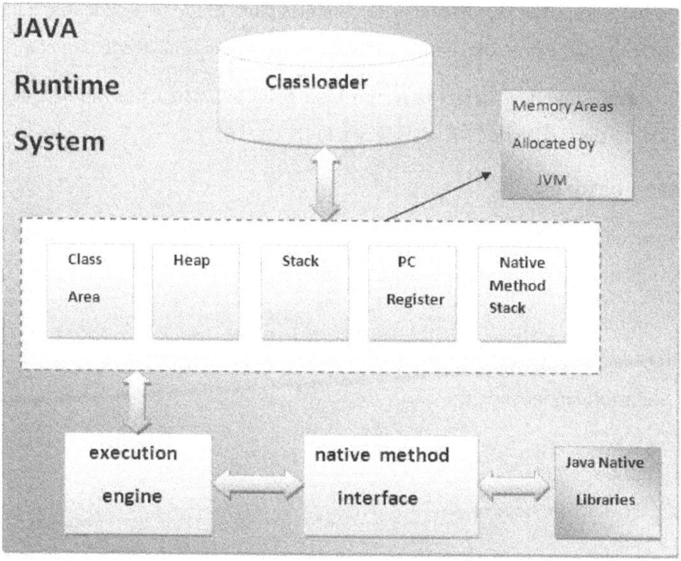


**4) Stack**

Java Stack stores frames .It holds local variables and partial results, and plays a part in method invocation and return.

Each thread has a private JVM stack, created at the same time as thread.

A new frame is created each time a method is invoked. A frame is destroyed when its method invocation completes.

**5) Program Counter Register**

PC (program counter) register. It contains the address of the Java virtual machine instruction currently being executed.

**6) Native Method Stack**

It contains all the native methods used in the application.

**7) Execution Engine**

It contains

- **Virtual processor**
- **Interpreter:** Read byte code stream then execute the instructions.
- **Just-In-Time (JIT) compiler**

It is used to improve the performance. JIT compiles parts of the byte code that have similar functionality at the same time, and hence reduces the amount of time needed for compilation.

Here the term? Compiler? Refers to a translator from the instruction set of a Java virtual machine (JVM) to the instruction set of a specific CPU.

## 1.8. Java Features

There is given many features of java. They are also known as java buzzwords. The Java Features given below are simple and easy to understand.

1. Simple
2. Object-Oriented
3. Platform independent
4. Secured
5. Robust
6. Architecture neutral
7. Portable
8. Dynamic
9. Interpreted
10. High Performance
11. Multithreaded
12. Distributed

### *Simple*

- According to Sun, Java language is simple because:
- Syntax is based on C++ (so easier for programmers to learn it after C++).
- Removed many confusing and/or rarely-used features e.g., explicit pointers, operator overloading etc.
- No Need to remove unreferenced objects because there is Automatic Garbage Collection in java.

### *Object-oriented*

Object-oriented means we organize our software as a combination of different types of objects that incorporates both data and behavior.

Object-oriented programming (OOPs) is a methodology that simplify software development and maintenance by providing some rules

Basic concepts of OOPs are:

1. Object
2. Class
3. Inheritance
4. Polymorphism
5. Abstraction
6. Encapsulation

### *Platform Independent*

A platform is the hardware or software environment in which a program runs. There are two types of platforms software-based and hardware-based. Java provides software-based platform.

The Java platform differs from most other platforms in the sense that it's a software-based platform that runs on top of other hardware-based platforms. It has two components:

1. Runtime Environment.
2. API (Application Programming Interface).

Java code can be run on multiple platforms e.g. Windows, Linux, Sun Solaris, and Mac/OS etc. Java code is compiled by the compiler and converted into byte code.

This byte code is a platform independent code because it can be run on multiple platforms i.e. Write Once and Run Anywhere (WORA).

### *Secured*

Java is secured because:

- No explicit pointer.
- Programs run inside virtual machine sandbox.

### *Robust*

Robust simply means strong. Java uses strong memory management. There is lack of pointers that avoids security problem.

There is automatic garbage collection in java. There is exception handling and type checking mechanism in java. All these points make java robust.

### *Architecture-neutral*

There is no implementation dependent feature e.g. size of primitive types is set.

### *Portable*

We may carry the java byte code to any platform.

### *High-performance*

Java is faster than traditional interpretation since byte code is "close" to native code still somewhat slower than a compiled language (e.g., C++).

### *Distributed*

We can create distributed applications in java. RMI and EJB are used for creating distributed applications. We may access files by calling the methods from any machine on the internet.

### *Multi-threaded*

A thread is like a separate program, executing concurrently. We can write Java programs that deal with many tasks at once by defining multiple threads. The main advantage of multi-threading is that it shares the same memory. Threads are important for multi-media, Web applications etc.

## 1.9. Program Structures

### *Description*

Let's use example of HelloWorld Java program to understand structure and features of class. This program is written on few lines, and its only task is to print "Hello World from Java" on the screen.

Refer the following picture:

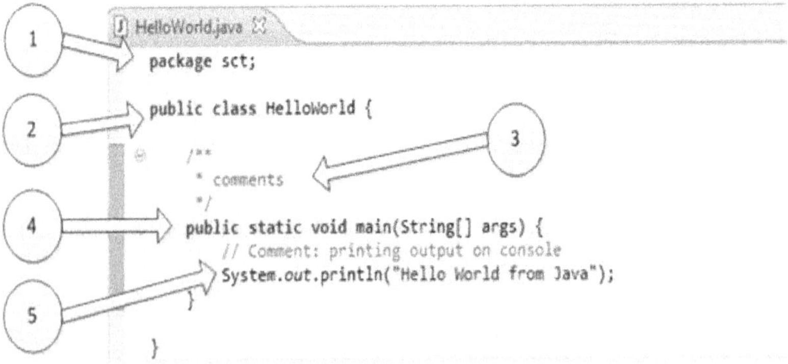

### *1. "package sct":*

It is package declaration statement. The package statement defines a name space in which classes are stored.

Package is used to organize the classes based on functionality. If you omit the package statement, the class names are put into the default package, which has no name. Package statement cannot appear anywhere in program. It must be first line of your program or you can omit it.

### *2. "public class HelloWorld":*

This line has various aspects of java programming.

a. **public**: This is access modifier keyword which tells compiler access to class. Various values of access modifiers can be public, protected, and private or default (no value).

b. **class**: This keyword used to declare class. Name of class (Hello World) followed by this keyword.

### *3. Comments Section*

We can write comments in java in two ways.

a. **Line comments**: It start with two forward slashes (//) and continue to the end of the current line. Line comments do not require an ending symbol.

b. **Block comments** start with a forward slash and an asterisk (/*) and end with an asterisk and a forward slash (*/).Block comments can also extend across as many lines as needed.

### *4. "public static void main (String [ ] args)"*

Its method (Function) named main with string array as argument.

a) **public** : Access Modifier

b) **static**: static is reserved keyword which means that a method is accessible and usable even though no objects of the class exist.

c) **void**: This keyword declares nothing would be returned from method. Method can return any primitive or object.

d) Method content inside curly braces. { }

### *5. System.out.println("Hello World from Java")*

a) **System**: It is name of Java utility class.

b) **out**: It is an object which belongs to System class.

c) **println**: It is utility method name which is used to send any String to console.

d) "Hello World from Java": It is String literal set as argument to println method.

## 1.10. Installation of JDK1.6

If you do not already have the JDK software installed or if JAVA_HOME is not set, the Java CAPS installation will not be successful.

The following tasks provide the information you need to install JDK software and set JAVA_HOME on UNIX or Windows systems.

### *Microsoft Windows*

JDK5: At least release 1.5.0_14

JDK6: At least release 1.6.0_03

Caution – It is not recommended to user JDK 1.6.0_13 or 1.6.0_14 with Java CAPS due to issues with several of the wizards used to develop applications. In addition, the installation fails on Windows when using JDK 1.6.0_13 or 1.6.0_14. The Java CAPS Installer does not support JDK release 1.6.0_04 in the 64-bit version on Solaris SPARC or AMD 64-bit environments. The installer also does not support JDK 1.6.0 or later on AIX 5.3.

### *▼To Install the JDK Software and Set JAVA_HOME on a Windows System*

1. Install the JDK software.
   a. Go to http://java.sun.com/javase/downloads/index.jsp.
   b. Select the appropriate JDK software and click Download.

   The JDK software is installed on your computer, for example, at C:\Program Files\Java\jdk1.6.0_02. You can move the JDK software to another location if desired.

2. To set JAVA_HOME:
   a. Right click My Computer and select Properties.
   b. On the Advanced tab, select Environment Variables, and then edit JAVA_HOME to point to where the JDK software is located, for example, C:\Program Files\Java\jdk1.6.0_02.

# CHAPTER II

# Classes & Objects

## 2.1. Variables

Variable is name of reserved area allocated in memory.

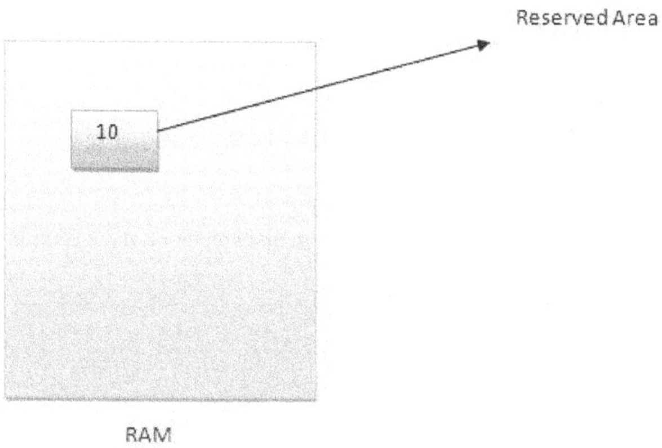


**Ex: int** data=50; //Here data is variable

### *Types of Variables*

There are three types of variables in java

- local variable
- instance variable
- static variable

### *Local Variable*

A variable that is declared inside the method is called local variable.

### *Instance Variable*

A variable that is declared inside the class but outside the method is called instance variable. It is not declared as static.

### *Static Variable*

A variable that is declared as static is called static variable. It cannot be local.

Example to understand the types of variables:

```
class A
{
    int data=50;//instance variable
    static int m=100;//static variable
    void method()
    {
        int n=90;//local variable
    }
}//end of class
```

## 2.2. Data Types

"Data types are used for representing the data in main memory of the computer.

In java, there are two types of data types:

- Primitive data types
- Non-primitive data types.

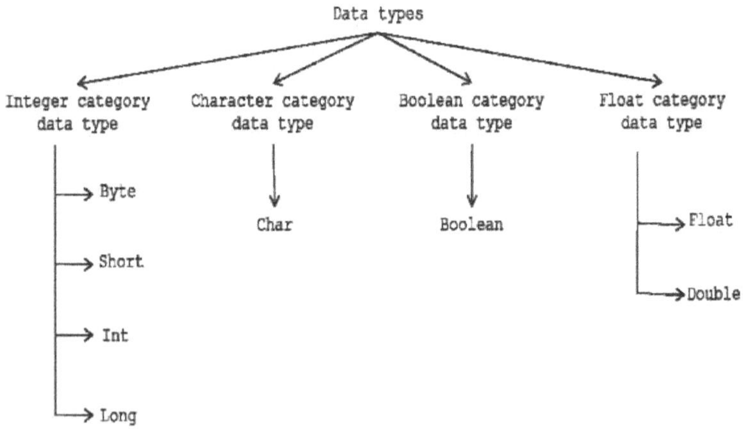


In JAVA, we have eight data types which are organized in four groups. They are integer category data types, float category data types, character category data types and Boolean category data types.

1. Integer category data types: These are used to represent integer data. This category of data type contains four data types which are given in the following table:

| Type | Contains | Default | Size | Range |
|---|---|---|---|---|
| byte | Signed integer | 0 | 8 bit or 1 byte | $-2^7$ to $2^7$-1 or -128 to 127 |
| short | Signed integer | 0 | 16 bit Or 2 bytes | $-2^{15}$ to $2^{15}$-1 or -32768 to 32767 |
| int | Signed integer | 0 | 32 bit Or 4 bytes | $-2^{31}$ to $2^{31}$-1 or -2147483648 to 2147483647 |
| long | Signed integer | 0L | 64 bit Or 8 bytes | $-2^{63}$ to $2^{63}$-1 or -9223372036854775808 to 9223372036854775807 |

2. Float category data types: Float category data types are used for representing the data in the form of scale, precision i.e., these category data types are used for representing float values. This category contains two data types; they are given in the following table:

| Type | Contains | Default | Size | Range | No of decimals |
|---|---|---|---|---|---|
| Float | IEEE 754 floating point single-precision | 0.0f | 32 Bit Or 4 bytes | 1.4E-45 to 3.4028235E+38 | 8 |
| double | IEEE 754 floating point double-precision | 0.0d | 64 Bit Or 8 bytes | 439E-324 to 1.7976931348623157E+308 | 16 |

3. CHAR

- Char data type is a single 16-bit Unicode character.
- Minimum value is '\u0000' (or 0).
- Maximum value is '\uffff' (or 65,535 inclusive).
- Char data type is used to store any character.
- Example: char letterA ='A'

## 2.3. Identifiers – Naming Conventions

Identifiers are symbolic names given to classes, methods and variables.

Identifiers should follow certain rules:

1. Identifiers can contain capital letters, small letters and numbers.

Examples of Valid identifiers:

Car; AnObject; myPROgrAM123

2. Identifiers can contain only the special characters Underscore (_), Dollar ($).

Examples of valid identifiers:

_aName; Student_Class; Student_; _$_$$_; $ant Invalid identifiers: Car>Class; %in;

3. Identifiers should not start with a number.

Ex: 1Plane; 1245

4. Identifiers should not contain spaces.

Ex: Student class; A class

5. Keywords cannot be used as identifiers.

Ex: class, for

6. Identifiers are case sensitive. Ex: Car, CAR, car, cAR, CaR

## 2.4. Keywords

**Keywords** are special tokens in the language which have reserved use in the language. Keywords may not be used as identifiers in Java — you cannot declare a field whose name is a keyword, for instance.

Examples of keywords are the primitive types, **int** and **boolean**; the control flow statements **for** and **if**; access modifiers such as **public**, and special words which mark the declaration and definition of Java classes, packages, and interfaces: **class, package, interface**.

Below are all the Java language keywords:

- **abstract**
- **assert** (since Java 1.4)
- **boolean**
- **break**
- **byte**
- **case**
- **catch**
- **char**
- **class**
- **const** (not used)
- **continue**
- **default**
- **do** ; **double**
- **else**
- **enum** (since Java 5.0)
- **extends**
- **final**
- **finally**
- **float**
- **for**
- **goto** (not used)
- **if**
- **implements**
- **import**
- **instanceof**
- **int**
- **interface**
- **long**
- **native**
- **new**
- **package**
- **private**
- **protected**
- **public**
- **return**
- **short**
- **static**
- **strictfp** (since Java 1.2)
- **super**

- **switch**
- **synchronized**
- **this**
- **throw**
- **throws**
- **transient**
- **try** ;
- **void;**
- **volatile;**
- **while.**

## 2.5. Literals

A literal is the source code representation of a fixed value. Literals in Java are a sequence of characters (digits, letters, and other characters) that represent constant values to be stored in variables. Java language specifies five major types of literals. Literals can be any number, text, or other information that represents a value.

This means what you type is what you get. We will use literals In addition to variables in Java statement. While writing a source code as a character sequence, we can specify any value as a literal such as an integer.

They are:

- **Integer literals**
- **Floating literals**

- **Character literals**
- **String literals**
- **Boolean literals**

Each of them has a type associated with it. The type describes how the values behave and how they are stored.

### *Integer Literals*

Integer data types consist of the following primitive data types: int, ong, byte, and short. Byte, int, long, and short can be expressed in decimal (base 10), hexadecimal (base 16) or octal (base 8) number systems as well.

Prefix 0 is used to indicate octal and prefix **0x** indicates hexadecimal when using these number systems for literals.

### *Examples*

**int decimal = 100;**

**int octal = 0144;**

**int hexa = 0x64;**

**Floating-point literals:**

Floating-point numbers are like real numbers in mathematics, for example, 4.13179, -0.000001.

Java has two kinds of floating-point numbers: float and double. The default type when you write a floating-point literal is double, but you can designate it explicitly by appending the D (or d) suffix. However, the suffix F (or f) is appended to designate the data type of a floating-point literal as float.

We can also specify a floating-point literal in scientific notation using Exponent (short E ore), for instance: the double literal 0.0314E2 is interpreted as: $0.0314 * 10^2$ (i.e 3.14). 6.5E+32 (or 6.5E32) Double-precision floating-point literal 7D Double-precision floating-point literal .01f Floating-point literal

### *Character Literals*

Char data type is a single 16-bit Unicode character. We can specify a character literal as a single printable character in a pair of single quote characters such as 'a', '#', and '3'. You must know about the ASCII character set. The ASCII character set includes 128 characters including letters, numerals, punctuation etc. Below table shows a set of these special characters.

| Escape | Meaning |
|---|---|
| \n | New line |
| \t | Tab |
| \b | Backspace |
| \r | Carriage return |
| \f | Formfeed |
| \\ | Backslash |
| \' | Single quotation mark |
| \" | Double quotation mark |
| \d | Octal |
| \xd | Hexadecimal |
| \ud | Unicode character |

If we want to specify a single quote, a backslash, or a non-Printable character as a character literal use an escape sequence.

An escape sequence uses a special syntax to represents a character.

The syntax begins with a single backslash character. You can see the below table to view the character literals use Unicode escape sequence to represent printable and non-printable characters.

| | |
|---|---|
| 'u0041' | Capital letter A |
| '\u0030' | Digit 0 |
| '\u0022' | Double quote " |
| '\u003b' | Punctuation ; |
| '\u0020' | Space |
| '\u0009' | Horizontal Tab |

### *String Literals*

The set of characters in represented as String literals in Java. Always use "double quotes" for String literals. There are few methods provided in Java to combine strings, modify strings and to know whether to strings have the same values.

| | |
|---|---|
| "" | The empty string |
| "\"" | A string containing |
| "This is a string" | A string containing 16 characters |
| "This is a " + "two-line string" | actually a string-valued constant expression, formed from two string literals |

### *Null Literals*

The final literal that we can use in Java programming is a Null literal. We specify the Null literal in the source code as 'null'.

To reduce the number of references to an object, use null literal.

The type of the null literal is always null. We typically assign null literals to object reference variables. For instance

s = null;

### *Boolean Literals*

The values true and false are treated as literals in Java programming. When we assign a value to a boolean variable, we can only use these two values.

Unlike C, We can't presume that the value of 1 is equivalent to true and 0 is equivalent to false in Java.

We have to use the values true and false to represent a Boolean value.

### *Example*

boolean chosen = true;

## 2.6. Java Operators

- In Java Variables are Value Container used to store some value.
- In order to Perform some **operation** on the Data we use different operators such as arithmetic Operator, Logical Operator etc.

### *Types of Operators*

1. Assignment Operator
2. Arithmetic Operator
3. Unary Operators
4. Relational Operator
5. Conditional Operators
6. Bitwise and Bit Shift Operators

## *Operators and its Precedence Table in Java*

| Operators | Precedence |
|---|---|
| postfix | ***expr++ expr--*** |
| unary | **++*expr* --*expr* +*expr* -*expr* ~ !** |
| multiplicative | * / % |
| additive | + - |
| shift | << >> >>> |
| relational | < > <= >= **instanceof** |
| equality | == != |
| bitwise AND | & |
| bitwise exclusive OR | ^ |
| bitwise inclusive OR | \| |
| logical AND | && |
| logical OR | \|\| |
| ternary | ? : |
| assignment | = += -= *= /= %= &= ^= \|= <<= >>= >>>= |

## *1. Java Assignment Operator*

- "=" is simple assignment operator in Java Programming.
  - "Assignment Operator" is binary Operator as it operates on two operands.
  - It have two values associated with it i.e Left Value and Right Value.
  - It is used to Assign Literal Value to the Variable.
  - Variable of Primitive Data Type
  - Array Variable
  - Object

### *Syntax and Example*

```
int javaProgramming; //Default Assignment 0 int
distance = 10; //Assign 10
int price = 1990; //Assign 1990
```

### *Ways of Assignment*

### *Way 1: Declare and Assign*

```
class AssignmentDemo {
   public static void main (String[] args){
      int ivar;
      ivar = 10;
      System.out.println(ivar);
   }
}
```

- Firstly we are going to declare variable of primitive data type.
- After declaring variable will have default value inside it (i.e 0).
- 10 is assigned to Variable "ivar".

### *Way 2: Declare and Assign in Single Statement*

```
class AssignmentDemo {
   public static void main (String[] args){
      int ivar = 10;
      System.out.println(ivar);
   }
}
```

### *Way 3: Assignment & Arithmetic Operation*

```
class AssignmentAndArithmetic {
   public static void main (String[] args){
      int num1 = 10;
      int num2 = 20;
      int num3 = num1 + num2;
      System.out.println(num1);
   }
}
```

## *2. Arithmetic Operators in Java Programming*

- The basic arithmetic operations in Java Programming are addition, subtraction, multiplication, and division.
- Arithmetic Operations are operated on Numeric Data Types as expected.

- Arithmetic Operators can be Overloaded.
- Arithmetic Operators are "Binary" Operators i.e they operates on two operands.

### *Arithmetic Operators used in Java*

| Operator | Use of Operator |
|---|---|
| + | Use to Add Two Numbers and Also used to Concatenate two strings |
| - | Used for Subtraction |
| * | Used to multiply numbers |
| / | Used for Division |
| % | Used for Finding Mod (Remainder Operator) |

### *Example 1: Arithmetic Operators*

```
class ArithmeticOperationsDemo {
   public static void main (String[] args){
      // answer is now 3
   int answer = 1 + 2;
   System.out.println(answer);
      // answer is now 2
      answer = answer - 1;
      System.out.println(answer);
    //  answer is now 4 answer =
      answer * 2;
      System.out.println(answer);
      // answer is now 2
      answer = answer / 2;
      System.out.println(answer);
      // answer is now 10
      answer = answer + 8;
      // answer is now 3
      answer = answer % 7;
      System.out.println(answer);
   }
}
```

*Example 2: Use of Modulus Operator*

```
class ModulusOperatorDemo {
 public static void main(String args[]) {
  int  x = 92;
  double y = 92.25;
 System.out.println("x mod 10 = " + x % 10);
 System.out.println("y mod 10 = " + y % 10);
 }
}
Output:
x mod 10 = 2
y mod 10 = 2.25
```

*Example: Arithmetic Compound Assignment Operators in Java*

```
class CompoundAssignmentDemo {
 public static void main(String args[]) {
  int a = 1;
  int b = 2;
  int c = 3;
  a += 1;
  b *= 1;
  c %= 1;
  System.out.println("a = " + a);
  System.out.println("b = " + b);
  System.out.println("c = " + c);
 }
}
```

*Output*

```
a = 2
b = 2
c = 0
```

### *3. Bitwise Operators in Java Programming*

- Java defines several bitwise operators, which can be applied to the integer types, long, int, short, char, and byte.
- Bitwise operator works on bits and performs bit-by-bit operation. Assume if a = 60; and b = 13; now in binary format they will be as follows:

**a = 0011 1100**

**b = 0000 1101**

-----------------

**a&b = 0000 1100**

**a|b = 0011 1101**

**a^b = 0011 0001**

**~a = 1100 0011**

| **Operator** | **Result** |
|---|---|
| ~ | Bitwise unary NOT |
| & | Bitwise AND |
| \| | Bitwise OR |
| ^ | Bitwise exclusive OR |
| >> | Shift right |

<table>
<tr><td>>>></td><td>Shift right zero fill</td></tr>
<tr><td><<</td><td>Shift left</td></tr>
<tr><td>&=</td><td>Bitwise AND assignment</td></tr>
<tr><td>|=</td><td>Bitwise OR assignment</td></tr>
<tr><td>^=</td><td>Bitwise exclusive OR assignment</td></tr>
<tr><td>>>=</td><td>Shift right assignment</td></tr>
<tr><td>>>>=</td><td>Shift right zero fill assignment</td></tr>
<tr><td><<=</td><td>Shift left assignment</td></tr>
</table>

### *Bitwise Operators: Bitwise unary NOT*

- Bitwise Unary Not is also called as bitwise complement.
- It is Unary Operator because it operates on single Operand.
- Unary Not Operator is denoted by – '~'.
- The Unary NOT operator inverts all of the bits of its operand.

### *Example 1: Bitwise unary NOT: Bitwise Operators*

```
class BitwiseNOT{
  public static void main(String args[]){
  int ivar =42;
  System.out.println("~ ivar = " + ~ivar);
  }
}
Output :
~ ivar = -43
```

### *Example 2: Unary Not Operator 0-5*

```
class BitwiseNOT{
  public static void main(String args[]){
  System.out.println("~ 0 = " + ~0);
  System.out.println("~ 1 = " + ~1);
  System.out.println("~ 2 = " + ~2);
  System.out.println("~ 3 = " + ~3);
    }
}
Output :
~ 0 = -1
~ 1 = -2
~ 2 = -3
~ 3 = -4
```

### *Bitwise AND Operator is,*

- Binary Operator as it Operates on 2 Operands.
- Denoted by – &
- Used for: Masking Bits.

### *Bitwise AND Summary Table*

| A | B | A & B |
|---|---|---|
| 0 | 0 | 0 |
| 0 | 1 | 0 |
| 1 | 0 | 0 |
| 1 | 1 | 1 |

### *Example 1: ANDing 42 and 15*

```
class BitwiseAND{
  public static void main(String args[]){
  int num1 = 42;
  int num2 = 15;
  System.out.println("AND Result =" +(num1&num2)); }
}
```

### *Output*

AND Result = 10

Explanation of Code :

Num1 : 00101010 42

Num2 : 00001111 15

=====================

AND : 00001010 10

42 is represented in Binary format as -> 00101010

15 is represented in Binary format as -> 00001111

According to above rule (table) we get 00001010 as final structure.

println method will print decimal equivalent of 00001010 and display it on screen.

### *Bitwise OR Operator is,*

- The OR operator, |, combines bits such that if either of the bits in the operands is a 1, then the resultant bit is a 1
- Binary Operator as it Operates on 2 Operands.
- Denoted by – |

*Bitwise OR Summary Table*

| A | B | A \| B |
|---|---|---|
| 0 | 0 | 0 |
| 0 | 1 | 1 |
| 1 | 0 | 1 |
| 1 | 1 | 1 |

*Example 1: ORing 42 and 15*

```
class BitwiseOR {
  public static void main(String args[]){
  int num1 = 42;
  int num2 = 15;
  System.out.println("OR Result =" +(num1 | num2));
  }
}
```

*Output*

```
OR Result = 47
```

*Explanation of Code*

Num1 : 00101010 42

Num2 : 00001111 15

=====================

OR : 00101111 47

42 is represented in Binary format as -> 00101010

15 is represented in Binary format as -> 00001111

According to above rule (table) we get 00101111 as final structure.

println method will print decimal equivalent of 00101111 and display it on screen.

*Bitwise XOR Operator is,*

- The XOR operator (^) combines bits such that if either of the bits in the operands is a 1, then the resultant bit is a 1
- Binary Operator as it Operates on 2 Operands.
- Denoted by : ^

### *Bitwise XOR Summary Table*

| A | B | A ^ B |
|---|---|---|
| 0 | 0 | 0 |
| 0 | 1 | 1 |
| 1 | 0 | 1 |
| 1 | 1 | 0 |

### *Example 1: XORing 42 and 15*

```
class BitwiseXOR {
  public static void main(String args[]){
  int num1 = 42;
  int num2 = 15;
  System.out.println("XOR Result =" +(num1 ^ num2));
  }
}
```

### *Output*

**XOR Result = 37**

**Explanation of Code:**

Num1 : 00101010 42

Num2 : 00001111 15

======================

XOR : 00100101 37

42 is represented in Binary format as -> 00101010

15 is represented in Binary format as -> 00001111

According to above rule (table) we get 00100101 as final structure.

println method will print decimal equivalent of 00100101 and display it on screen.

### *Bit Shift Operator in Java*

- The bitwise shift operators take two operands.

- The first is a quantity to be shifted, and the second specifies the number of bit positions by which the first operand is to be shifted.
- The direction of the shift operation is controlled by the operator used. Shift operators convert their operands to 32 or 64 bits and return a result of the same type as the left operator.

| Shift Operators | | | |
|---|---|---|---|
| **Operator** | **Name** | **Use** | **Description** |
| << | Shift left | **op1 << op2** | Shifts bits of op1 left by distance op2; fills with 0 bits on the right side |
| >> | Shift right | **op1 >> op2** | Shifts bits of op1 right by distance op2; fills with highest (sign) bit on the left side |
| >>> | Shift right zero fill | **op1 >> op2** | Shifts bits of op1 right by distance op2; fills with 0 bits on the left side |

Shifting is basically taking the binary equivalent of a number and moving the bit pattern left or right.

### *Example*

```
class Bit{
public static void main(String []args)
{
int a =2;
System.out.println(" rightshift by 1 is:" +(a>>1));
System.out.println(" leftshift by 1 is:" +(a<<1));
System.out.println(" Shift right zero fill by 1 is:" +(a>>1));
}
}
```

### *Out Put*

```
C:\>javac Bit.java
C:\>java Bit
 rightshift by 1 is:leftshift by 1 is:4
 Shift right zero fill by 1 is: 1
```

**Example:** Bitwise AND assignment, Bitwise OR assignment, Bitwise exclusive OR assignment, Shift right assignment, Shift right zero fill assignment and Shift left assignment

```
public class Bitwise_assign {
 public static void main(String args[]) {
  int a = 1;
  int b = 2;
  int c = 3;
  a |= 4;
  b >>= 1;
  c <<= 1;
  a ^= c;
  System.out.println("a = " + a);
  System.out.println("b = " + b);
  System.out.println("c = " + c);
 }
}
```

*OutPut*

```
C:\>javac Bitwise_assign.java
C:\>java Bitwise_assign
a = 3
b = 1
c = 6
```

### *4.Unary Operators in Java Programming*

- The unary operators require only one operand.
- There are 5 unary operators in Java Programming Language.
- Unary Operators are:
  - Unary Plus
  - Unary Minus
  - Logical Compliment Operator
  - Increment Operator
  - Decrement Operator

*Example: Unary Operator*

```
class UnaryDemo {
  public static void main(String[] args){
     //  result is now 1
  int result = +1;
  System.out.println(result);
     //  result is now -1
     result = -result;
     System.out.println(result);
     // false
     boolean success = false;
     System.out.println(success);
     //  true
     System.out.println(
     !success);
  }
 }
```

**Out Put:**

```
C:\>javac UnaryDemo.java
C:\>java UnaryDemo
1
-1
false
true
```

### *Increment and Decrement Operator in Java*

- It is one of the variation of "Arithmetic Operator".
- Increment and Decrement Operators are Unary Operators.
- Unary Operator Operates on One Operand.
- Increment Operator is Used to Increment Value Stored inside Variable on which it is operating.
- Decrement Operator is used to decrement value of Variable by 1 (default).

### *Types of Increment and Decrement Operator*

- Pre Increment / Pre Decrement Operator
- Post Increment / Post Decrement Operator

*Syntax*

++ Increment operator : increments a value by 1 -- Decrement operator : decrements a value by 1

***Example***

```
class Inc_Dec {
  public static void main(String args[]) {
    int num1 = 1;
    int num2 = 1;
    num1++;
    num2++;
    System.out.println("num1 = " + num1);
    System.out.println("num2 = " + num2);
    ++num1;
    ++num2;
    System.out.println("num1 = " + num1);
    System.out.println("num2 = " + num2);
    num1--;
    num2--;
    System.out.println("num1 = " + num1);
    System.out.println("num2 = " + num2);
    --num1;
    --num2;
    System.out.println("num1 = " + num1);
    System.out.println("num2 = " + num2);
     }
}
```

***OutPut***

```
C:\>javac Inc_Dec.java
C:\>java Inc_Dec
num1 = 2
num2 = 2
num1 = 3
num2 = 3
```

num1 = 2

num2 = 2

num1 = 1

num2 = 1

### *5. Logical Operators*

Every programming language has its own logical operators, or at least a way of expressing logic. Java's logical operators are split into two subtypes, relational and conditional.

### *Relational Operators in Java Programming*

- Relational Operators are used to check relation between two variables or numbers.
- Relational Operators are Binary Operators.
- Relational Operators returns "Boolean" value .i.e it will return true or false.
- Most of the relational operators are used in "If statement" and inside Looping statement in order to check truthness or falseness of condition.

| Operator | Use | Description |
|---|---|---|
| > | op1 > op2 | op1 is greater than op2 |
| >= | op1 >= op2 | op1 is greater than or equal to op2 |
| < | op1 < op2 | op1 is less than op2 |
| <= | op1 <= op2 | op1 is less than or equal to op2 |
| == | op1 == op2 | op1 and op2 are equal |
| != | op1 != op2 | op1 and op2 are not equal |

### *Logical Operators*

There are four logical operators in Java, however one of them is less commonly used and I will not discuss here. It's really optional compared to the ones I will introduce, and these will be a whole heck of a lot useful to you now.

Here's your table of logical operators:

| Conditional symbols and their meanings | |
|---|---|
| Symbol | Condition |
| && | AND |
| \|\| | OR |
| ! | NOT |

*Example*

```
public class MainClass {
  public static void main(String[] args) {
    int i = 5;
    int j = 6;
    System.out.println("i = " + i);
    System.out.println("j = " + j);
    System.out.println("i > j is " + (i > j));
    System.out.println("i < j is " + (i < j));
    System.out.println("i >= j is " + (i >= j));
    System.out.println("i <= j is " + (i <= j));
    System.out.println("i == j is " + (i == j));
    System.out.println("i != j is " + (i != j));
    System.out.println("(i < 10) && (j < 10) is " + ((i < 10) && (j < 10)));
    System.out.println("(i < 10) || (j < 10) is " + ((i < 10) || (j < 10)));
  }
}
```

*Out Put*

```
C:\>javac MainClass.java
C:\>java MainClass
i = 5
j = 6
i > j is false
i < j is true
i >= j is false
i <= j is true
i == j is false
i != j is true
(i < 10) && (j < 10) is true
(i < 10) || (j < 10) is true
```

### *6. Ternary Operator*

Ternary operator is also known as the Conditional operator. This operator consists of three operands and is used to evaluate Boolean expressions.

The goal of the operator is to decide which value should be assigned to the variable. The operator is written as:

**variable x = (expression) ? value if true : value if false**

*Example*

```
public class Ternary {
  public static void main(String args[]){
    int a, b;
    a = 10;
    b = (a == 1) ? 20: 30;
    System.out.println( "Value of b is : " + b );
    b = (a == 10) ? 20: 30;
    System.out.println( "Value of b is : " + b );
  }
}
```

*OutPut*

```
C:\>javac Ternary.java
C:\>java Ternary
Value of b is : 30
Value of b is : 20
```

## 2.7. Expressions

- An expression is a construct made up of variables, operators, and method invocations, which are constructed according to the syntax of the language that evaluates to a single value.
- Examples of expressions are in bold below:
  a. int number = 0;
  b. int anArray[0] = 100;
  c. System.out.println ("Element 1 at index 0: " + anArray[0]);
  d. int result = 1 + 2; // result is now 3 if(value1 == value2)
  c. System.out.println ("value1 == value2");
- The data type of the value returned by an expression depends on the elements used in the expression.

- The expression number = 0 returns an int because the assignment operator returns a value of the same data type as its left-hand operand; in this case, number is an int.
- As you can see from the other expressions, an expression can return other types of values as well, such as boolean or String.
- The Java programming language allows you to construct compound expressions from various smaller expressions as long as the data type required by one part of the expression matches the data type of the other.
- Here's an example of a compound expression: 1 * 2 * 3.

## 2.8. Precedence and Associativity Rules for Operators

Precedence and associativity rules are necessary for deterministic evaluation of expressions.

- The operators are shown with decreasing precedence from the top of the table.
- Operators within the same row have the same precedence.
- Parentheses, ( ), can be used to override precedence and associativity.
- The unary operators, which require one operand, include the postfix increment (++) and decrement (--) operators from the first row, all the prefix operators (+, -, ++, --, ~, !) in the second row, and the prefix operators (object creation operator new, cast operator (type)) in the third row.
- The conditional operator (? :) is ternary, that is, requires three operands.
- All operators not listed above as unary or ternary, are binary, that is, require two operands.
- All binary operators, except for the relational and assignment operators, associate from left to right. The relational operators are nonassociative.
- Except for unary postfix increment and decrement operators, all unary operators, all assignment operators, and the ternary conditional operator associate from right to left.
- Precedence rules are used to determine which operator should be applied first if there are two operators with different precedence, and these follow each other in the expression. In such a case, the operator with the highest precedence is applied first.
- 2 + 3 * 4 is evaluated as 2 + (3 * 4) (with the result 14) since * has higher precedence than +.

- Associativity rules are used to determine which operator should be applied first if there are two operators with the same precedence, and these follow each other in the expression.
- Left associativity implies grouping from left to right:
- 1 + 2 - 3 is interpreted as ((1 + 2) - 3), since the binary operators + and - both have same precedence and left associativity.
- Right associativity implies grouping from right to left:
- - - 4 is interpreted as (- (- 4)) (with the result 4), since the unary operator - has right associativity.
- The precedence and associativity rules together determine the evaluation order of the operators.

### *Evaluation Order of Operands*

In order to understand the result returned by an operator, it is important to understand the evaluation order of its operands. Java states that the operands of operators are evaluated from left to right.

Java guarantees that all operands of an operator are fully evaluated before the operator is applied. The only exceptions are the short-circuit conditional operators &&, ||, and ?:.

In the case of a binary operator, if the left-hand operand causes an exception the right-hand operand is not evaluated.

The evaluation of the left-hand operand can have side effects that can influence the value of the right-hand operand. For example, in the following code:

```
int b = 10;
System.out.println((b=3) + b);
```

The value printed will be 6 and not 13. The evaluation proceeds as follows:

```
(b=3) + b
 3 + b b is assigned the value 3
 3 + 3
 6
```

The evaluation order also respects any parentheses, and the precedence and associativity rules of operators. Examples illustrating how the operand evaluation order influences the result returned by an operator.

| Operator | Description | Level | Associativity |
|---|---|---|---|
| []<br>.<br>()<br>++<br>-- | access array element<br>access object member<br>invoke a method<br>post-increment<br>post-decrement | 1 | left to right |
| ++<br>--<br>+<br>-<br>!<br>~ | pre-increment<br>pre-decrement<br>unary plus<br>unary minus<br>logical NOT<br>bitwise NOT | 2 | right to left |
| ()<br>new | cast<br>object creation | 3 | right to left |
| *<br>/<br>% | Multiplicative | 4 | left to right |
| + -<br>+ | additive<br>string concatenation | 5 | left to right |
| << >><br>>>> | Shift | 6 | left to right |
| < <=<br>> >=<br>Instance of | relational<br>type comparison | 7 | left to right |

| | | | |
|---|---|---|---|
| == != | Equality | 8 | left to right |
| | | | |
| & | bitwise AND | 9 | left to right |
| | | | |
| ^ | bitwise XOR | 10 | left to right |
| | | | |
| \| | bitwise OR | 11 | left to right |
| | | | |
| && | conditional AND | 12 | left to right |
| | | | |
| \|\| | conditional OR | 13 | left to right |
| ?: | Conditional | 14 | right to left |
| = += -= *= /= %= &= ^= \|= | Assignment | 15 | right to left |

## 2.9. Java Data Type Casting Type Conversion

**Summary:** By the end of this tutorial "Java Data Type Casting Type Conversion", you will be comfortable with converting one data type to another either implicitly or explicitly.

Java supports two types of castings – **primitive data type casting** and **reference type casting**. **Reference** type casting is nothing but assigning one Java object to another object. It comes with very strict rules and is explained clearly in Object Casting. Now let us go for data type casting. Java data type casting comes with 3 flavors.

1. **Implicit casting**
2. **Explicit casting**
3. **Boolean casting.**

### *1. Implicit Casting (Widening Conversion)*

**A data type of lower size (occupying less memory) is assigned to a data type of higher size**. This is done implicitly by the JVM. The lower size is widened to higher size. This is also named as **automatic type conversion**.

*Examples*

```
int x = 10;                  // occupies 4 bytes
double y = x;                // occupies 8 bytes
System.out.println(y);       // prints 10.0
```

In the above code 4 bytes integer value is assigned to 8 bytes double value.

byte → short → int → long → float → double

widening →

*Example*

```
public class Test
{
    public static void main(String[] args)
                {
    int i = 100;
    long l = i;     //no explicit type casting required
    float f = l;    //no explicit type casting required
    System.out.println("Int value "+i);
    System.out.println("Long value "+l);
    System.out.println("Float value "+f);
    }
}
```

*Out Put*

```
Int value 100
Long value 100
Float value 100.0
```

## 2. *Explicit Casting (Narrowing Conversion)*

A data type of higher size (occupying more memory) cannot be assigned to a data type of lower size. This is not done implicitly by the JVM and requires **explicit casting**; a casting operation to be performed by the programmer. The higher size is narrowed to lower size.

```
double x = 10.5;          // 8 bytes
int y = x;                // 4 bytes ; raises compilation error
```

In the above code, 8 bytes double value is narrowed to 4 bytes int value. It raises error. Let us explicitly type cast it.

```
double x = 10.5;
 int y = (int) x;
```

The double **x** is explicitly converted to int **y**. The thumb rule is, on both sides, the same data type should exist.

double → float → long → int → short → byte

**Narrowing** →

```
public class Test
{
   public static void main(String[] args)
   {
     double d = 100.04;
     long l = (long)d; //explicit type casting required
     int i = (int)l; //explicit type casting required
     System.out.println("Double value "+d);
     System.out.println("Long value "+l);
     System.out.println("Int value "+i);
      }
   }
```

Out Put:

Double value 100.04

Long value 100

Int value 100

## 3. *Boolean Casting*

A boolean value cannot be assigned to any other data type. Except boolean, all the remaining 7 data types can be assigned to one another either implicitly or explicitly; but boolean cannot.

We say, boolean is **incompatible** for conversion. Maximum we can assign a boolean value to another boolean.

Following raises error.

```
boolean x = true;
      int y = x;                    // error
      boolean x = true;
      int y = (int) x;              // error
byte -> short -> int -> long -> float -> double
```

**In the above statement, left to right can be assigned implicitly and right to left requires explicit casting. That is,** byte **can be assigned to** short **implicitly but** short **to** byte **requires explicit casting.**

*Following char operations are possible*

```
public class Demo
{
  public static void main(String args[])
  {
    char ch1 = 'A';
    double d1 = ch1;
    System.out.println(d1);              // prints 65.0
    System.out.println(ch1 * ch1);       // prints 4225 , 65 * 65
    double d2 = 66.0;
    char ch2 = (char) d2;
    System.out.println(ch2);             // prints B
  }
}
```

Pass your comments for the betterment of this tutorial "Java Data Type Casting Type Conversion". Your one stop destination for all data type conversions.

| **byte TO** | short | int | long | float | double | char | boolean |
|---|---|---|---|---|---|---|---|
| **short TO** | byte | int | long | float | double | char | boolean |
| **int TO** | byte | short | long | float | double | char | boolean |
| **float TO** | byte | short | int | long | double | char | boolean |
| **double TO** | byte | short | int | long | float | char | boolean |
| **char TO** | byte | short | int | long | float | double | boolean |
| **boolean TO** | byte | short | int | long | float | double | char |

*String and Data Type Conversions*

| **String TO** | byte | short | int | long | float | double | char | boolean |
|---|---|---|---|---|---|---|---|---|
| byte | short | int | long | float | double | char | boolean | **TO String** |

## 2.10. Java Control Flow Statements

- All the programs we have written till now had a sequential flow of control i.e. the statements were executed line by line from the top to bottom in an order.
- Nowhere were any statements skipped or a statement executed more than once. We will now look into how this can be achieved using control structures.
- Java control statements cause the flow of execution to advance and branch based on the changes to the state of the program.
- Control statements are divided into three groups:
    - ***selection*** statements allow the program to choose different parts of the execution based on the outcome of an expression
    - ***iteration*** statements enable program execution to repeat one or more statements
    - ***jump*** statements enable your program to execute in a non-linear fashion

***Selection Statements or Conditional Statements***

- Java selection statements allow to control the flow of program's execution based upon conditions known only during run-time.
- Java provides four selection statements:
    1. if
    2. if-else
    3. if-else-if
    4. switch

***if***

Statement(s) between the set of curly braces '{ }' will be executed only if the condition(s), between the set of brackets '( )' after 'if' keyword, is/are true.

***Syntax:***

```
if (Condition) {
    // statements;
}
```

*if-else*

If the condition(s) between the brackets '( )' after the 'if' keyword is/are true then the statement(s) between the immediately following set of curly braces '{ }' will be executed else the statement(s) under, the set of curly braces after the 'else' keyword will be executed.

***Example:***

***Syntax:***

```
            if (condition) {
        // statements;
      }
       else {
        // statements;}
class Example_if_else
{
    public static void main(String Args[])
    {
        if( a > b)
        {
                System.out.println("A = " + a + "\tB =
                " + b); System.out.println("A is
                greater than B");
        }
        else
        {
                System.out.println("A = " + a + "\tB = " + b);
                System.out.println("Either both are equal or B is
                greater");
        }
    }
}
class Example_nested_if _else
{
   public static void main(String Args[])
   {
```

```
        int a = 3;
         if (a <= 10 && a > 0)
         {
                System.out.println("Number is valid.");
                if ( a < 5)
                        System.out.println("From 1 to 5");
                else
                        System.out.println("From 5 to 10");
         }
        else
            System.out.println("Number is not valid");
    }
}
class Example_if_elseif_else
{
   public static void main (String Args[])
   {
        int a = 5;
        boolean val = false;
         if(val )
                System.out.println("val is false, so it won't
        execute"; else if (a < 0 )
                System.out.println("A is a negative
        value"); else if (a > 0)
                System.out.println ("A is a positive value");
        else
                System.out.println ("A is equal to zero");
   }
}
```

**switch**

When there is a long list of cases & conditions, then if/if-else is not good choice as the code would become complicated.

*Syntax*

```
switch (expression)
{
  case value1:
  //statement;
  break;
  case value2:
  //statement;
  break;
  default:
   //statement;
}
```

The moment user enters his choice, it will be matched with the cases' names & program execution will jump to the matching 'Case' & the statement under that case will be executed till the keyword 'break' comes. It is very important else the other unwanted cases will also get executed. After the last case there is 'default' keyword. Statements between 'default:' and the closing bracket of switch-case region will be executed only if the user has entered any wrong value as his choice i.e. other than the cases' names.

*Example Program*

```
class Example_switch
{
    public static void main(String Args[])
   {
      int month = 3;

      switch (month)
      {
      case 1:
            System.out.println("The month of
            January"); break;
      case 2:
            System.out.println("The month of
            February"); break;
      case 3:
```

```
            System.out.println("The month of
            March"); break;
        case 4:
            System.out.println("The month of April");
            break;
        case 5:
            System.out.println("The month of May");
            break;
        case 6:
            System.out.println("The month of June");
            break;
        case 7:
            System.out.println("The month of July");
            break;
        case 8:
            System.out.println("The month of August");
            break;
        case 9:
            System.out.println("The month of September");
             break;
        case 10:
            System.out.println("The month of October");
            break;
        case 11:
            System.out.println("The month of November");
            break;
        case 12:
            System.out.println("The month of December");
            break;
        default:
            System.out.println("Invalid month");
        }
    }
}
```

## 2.11. Iterative Statement (Loop Control Statement)

- There may be a situation when you need to execute a block of code several number of times. In general, statements are executed sequentially: The first statement in a function is executed first, followed by the second, and so on.
- Programming languages provide various control structures that allow for more complicated execution paths.
- A **loop** statement allows us to execute a statement or group of statements multiple times and following is the general form of a loop statement in most of the programming languages:

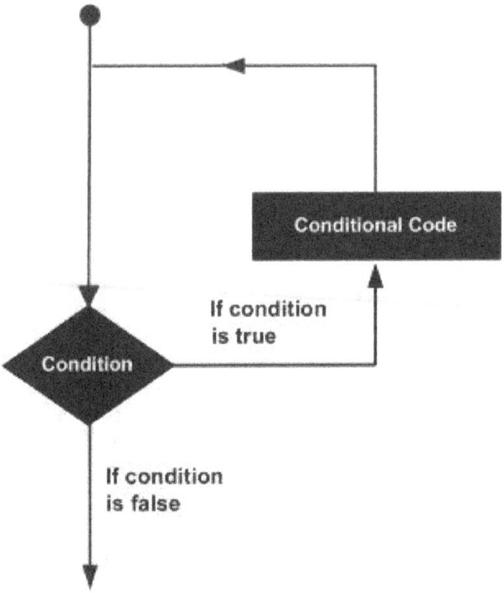


***For Loop in Java Programming***

- For Loop is one of the looping statement in java programming.
- For Loop is used to execute set of statements repeatedly until the condition is true.
- For Loop checks the contrition and executes the set of the statements , It is loop control statement in java.
- For Loop contain the following statements such as "**Initialization**", "**Condition**" and "**Increment/Decrement**" statement.

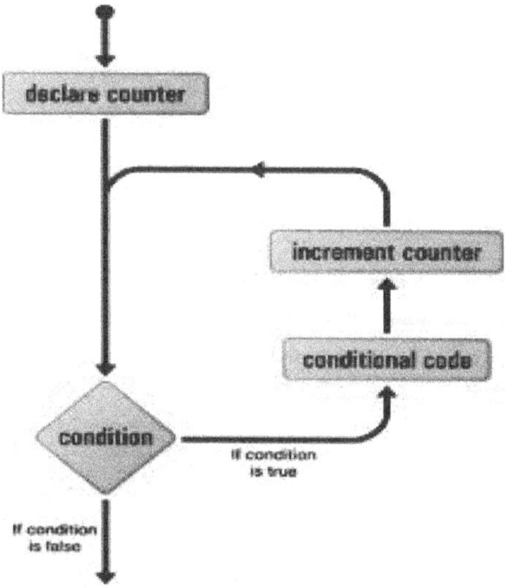


*Example: For Loop Statement*

```
class ForDemo {
        public static void main(String[] args){
            for(int i=1; i<11; i++){
                System.out.println("Count is : " + i);
            }
        }
}
```

*Output*

```
Count is: 1
Count is: 2
Count is: 3
Count is: 4
Count is: 5
Count is: 6
Count is: 7
Count is: 8
Count is: 9
Count is: 10
```

*While Loop Statement in Java*

- In java "**while**" is iteration statements like for and do-while.
- It is also called as "**Loop Control Statement**".
- "**While Statement**" repeatedly executes the same set of instructions until a termination condition is met.
- While loop is **Entry Controlled Loop** because condition is check at the entrance.
- If initial condition is true then and then only control enters into the while loop body
- In for loop initialization, condition and increment all three statements are combined into the one statement , in "**while loop**" all these statements are written **as separate statements**.
- Conditional Expression written inside while must **return boolean value**.

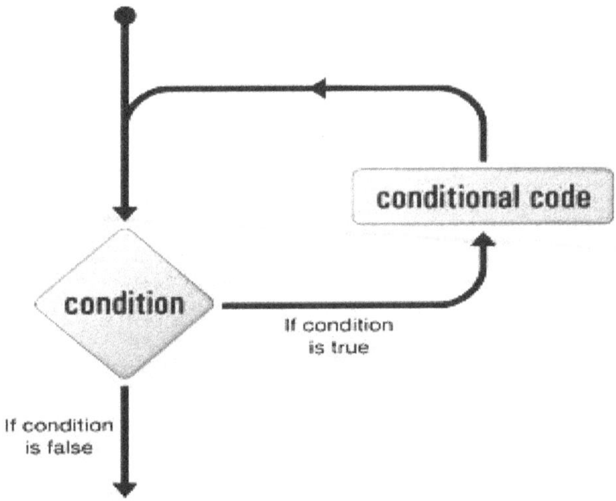


*Syntax*

```
while(condition) {
  // body of loop
}
```

- The condition is any Boolean expression.
- The body of the loop will be executed as long as the conditional expression is true.
- When condition becomes false, control passes to the next line of code immediately following the loop.
- The curly braces are unnecessary if only a single statement is being repeated.

*Example*

```
class WhileDemo {
  public static void main(String[] args){
    int cnt = 1;
    while (cnt < 11) {
      System.out.println("Number Count : " + cnt);
      count++;
    }
  }
}
```

*Java do-while Loop*

- In java "**Do-while**" is iteration statements like for loop and while loop.
- It is also called as "**Loop Control Statement**".
- "**Do-while Statement**" is **Exit Controlled Loop** because condition is check at the last moment.
- Irrespective of the condition, control enters into the do-while loop , after completion of body execution, condition is checked whether true/false. If condition is false then it will jump out of the loop.
- Conditional Expression written inside while must **return boolean value**.
- In do-while loop body gets executed once whatever may be the condition but condition must be true if you need to execute body for second time.

*Syntax: Do-While Loop*

```
do {
    Statement1;
    Statement2;
    Statement3;
    ..
    .
    StatementN;
} while (expression);
```

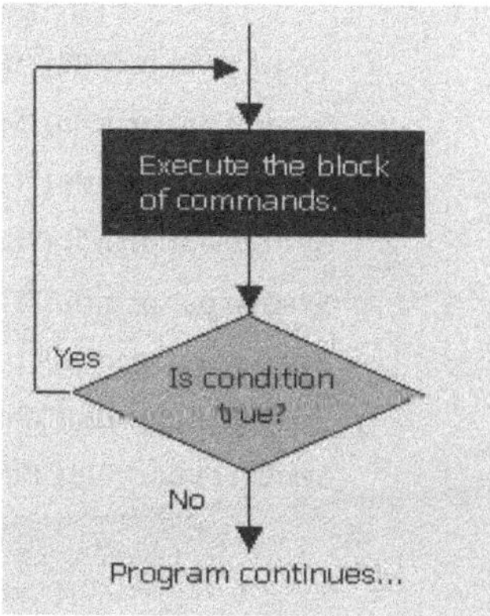

*Example 1: Printing Numbers*

```
class DoWhile {
public static void main(String
 args[]) { int n = 5;
 do
 {
  System.out.println("Sample
  : " + n); n--;
  }while(n > 0);
}
```

***Programs***

1. *Write a JAVA program to display default value of all primitive data types of JAVA*

```
class DefaultValues
{
    static byte b;
    static short s;
    static int i;
    static long l;
    static float f;
    static double d;
    static char c;
    static boolean bl;
    public static void main(String[] args)
    {
        System.out.println("Byte :"+b);
        System.out.println("Short :"+s);
        System.out.println("Int :"+i);
        System.out.println("Long :"+l);
        System.out.println("Float :"+f);
        System.out.println("Double :"+d);
        System.out.println("Char :"+c);
        System.out.println("Boolean :"+bl);
    }
}
```

**Out Put**

```
E:\JAVA>javac DefaultValues.java
E:\JAVA>java DefaultValues
Byte :0
Short :0
Int :0
Long :0
Float :0.0
Double :0.0
Char :
Boolean :false
```

2. *Write a JAVA program to get the minimum and maximum value of a primitive data types*

```
public class MinMaxExample
{
 public static void main(String[] args)
 {
  System.out.println("Byte.MIN = " + Byte.MIN_VALUE);
  System.out.println("Byte.MAX = " + Byte.MAX_VALUE);
  System.out.println("Short.MIN = " + Short.MIN_VALUE);
  System.out.println("Short.MAX = " + Short.MAX_VALUE);
  System.out.println("Integer.MIN = " +
  Integer.MIN_VALUE); System.out.println("Integer.MAX = "
  + Integer.MAX_VALUE); System.out.println("Long.MIN = "
  + Long.MIN_VALUE); System.out.println("Long.MAX = " +
  Long.MAX_VALUE); System.out.println("Float.MIN = " +
  Float.MIN_VALUE); System.out.println("Float.MAX = " +
  Float.MAX_VALUE); System.out.println("Double.MIN = " +
  Double.MIN_VALUE); System.out.println("Double.MAX = "
  + Double.MAX_VALUE);
 }
}
```

***Out Put***

```
E:\JAVA>javac MinMaxExample.java
E:\JAVA>java MinMaxExample
Byte.MIN = -128
```

```
Byte.MAX = 127
Short.MIN = -32768
Short.MAX = 32767
Integer.MIN = -2147483648
Integer.MAX = 2147483647
Long.MIN = -9223372036854775808
Long.MAX = 9223372036854775807
Float.MIN = 1.4E-45
Float.MAX = 3.4028235E38
Double.MIN = 4.9E-324
Double.MAX = 1.7976931348623157E308
```

3. *Write a JAVA program to display the Fibonacci sequence*

```
class FibonacciExample1{
public static void main(String args[])
{
int n1=0,n2=1,n3,i,count=10;
System.out.print(n1+""+n2);
for(i=2;i<count;++i)
 {
  n3=n1+n2;
  System.out.print
  (" "+n3); n1=n2;
  n2=n3;
 }
  }
}
```

***Out Put***

```
E:\JAVA>javac FibonacciExample1.java
E:\JAVA>java FibonacciExample1
0   1 1 2 3 5 8 13 21 34
```

4. *Write a JAVA program give example for command line arguments.*

```
class CommandLineExample
{
```

```
public static void main(String args[]){
System.out.println("Your first argument is: "+args[0]);
System.out.println("Your first argument is: "+args[1]);
System.out.println("Your first argument is: "+args[2]);
}
}
```

***Out Put***

```
E:\JAVA>javac CommandLineExample.java E:\JAVA>java
CommandLineExample PACE prakasam cse
Your first argument is: PACE
Your first argument is: prakasam
Your first argument is: cse
```

5. *Write java Program which is capable of adding any number of integers passed as command line arguments.*

```
public class Add {
    public static void main(String[] args) {
        int sum = 0;
        for (int i = 0; i < args.length; i++) {
            sum = sum + Integer.parseInt(args[i]);
        }
        System.out.println("The sum of the arguments passed is " + sum);
    }
}
```

***OutPut***

```
E:\JAVA>javac Add.java
E:\JAVA>java Add 1 2 5
The sum of the arguments passed is 8
```

## 2.12. Jump Statements

- Java jump statements enable transfer of control to other parts of program.
- Java provides three jump statements:

a. break

b. continue

c. return

- In addition, Java supports exception handling that can also alter the control flow of a program.
- Java programs.

### *Continue Statement in Java*

Continue Statement in Java is used to skip the part of loop. Unlike break statement it does not terminate the loop, instead it skips the remaining part of the loop and control again goes to check the condition again.

### *Syntax*

```
{
//loop body
-----------
-----------
-----------
continue;
----------
-----------
}
```

- Continue Statement is **Jumping Statement in Java Programming** like break.
- Continue Statement skips the Loop and **Re-Executes Loop with new condition**.
- Continue Statement **can be used only in Loop Control Statements** such as For Loop | While Loop | do-While Loop.
- **Continue** is Keyword in Java Programming.

### *Example*

```
public class continue_demo {
    public static void main(String[] args) {
        int j;
        for (j = 1; j < 5; j++) {
            if (j == 3) {
                System.out.println("continue!");
```

```
                    continue;
                    }
                    System.out.println(j);
                }
            }
        }
```

*Out Put*

```
C:\>java continue_demo
1
2
continue!
4
```

***Return Statement in Java***

- Return statement in used to explicitly return from a method. Return causes program control to transfer back to the caller of the method.
- The return statement immediately terminates the method in which it is executed.
- We can specify return type of the method as **"Primitive Data Type" or "Class name"**.
- Return Type can be "Void" means **it does not return any value**.
- Method can return a value by using "**return**" keyword.

***Syntax***

```
return;
```

## 2.13. Classes

- Class is a template for creating objects which defines its **state** and **behavior**. A class contains *field* and *method* to define the *state* and behavior of its object.
- In Java everything is encapsulated under classes. Class is the core of Java language.
- Class can be defined as a template/ blueprint that describe the behaviors /states of a particular entity.
- A class defines new data type. Once defined this new type can be used to create object of that type. Object is an instance of class. You may also call it as physical existence of a logical template class.

- A class is declared using **class** keyword. A class contain both data and code that operate on that data. The data or variables defined within a **class** are called **instance variables** and the code that operates on this data is known as **methods**.
- A class in java can contain:
    a. **data member**
    b. **method**
    c. **constructor**
    d. **block**
    e. **class and interface**

### *Rules for Java Class*

- A class can have only public or default(no modifier) access specifier.
- It can be either abstract, final or concrete (normal class).
- It must have the class keyword, and class must be followed by a legal identifier.
- It may optionally extend one parent class. By default, it will extend java.lang.Object.
- It may optionally implement any number of comma-separated interfaces.
- The class's variables and methods are declared within a set of curly braces {} .
- Each **.java** source file may contain only one public class. A source file may contain any number of default visible classes.
- Finally, the source file name must match the public class name and it must have a .java suffix.
- By convention, class names capitalize the initial of each word.
- For example: Employee, Boss, DateUtility, PostOffice, RegularRateCalculator.
- This type of naming convention is known as Pascal naming convention.
- The other convention, the camel naming convention, capitalize the initial of each word, except the first word.
- Method and field names use the camel naming convention.

### *Syntax to Declare*

**a class:**

***class <class_name>***

```
{
    data member;
    method;
}
```

*Example*

```
class Student.
{
 String name;
 int rollno;
 int age;
}
```

## 2.14. Object in Java

- An entity that has state and behavior is known as an object e.g. chair, bike, marker, pen, table, car etc. It can be physical or logical (tengible and intengible). The example of integible object is banking system.
- An object has three characteristics:
  - **state:** represents data (value) of an object.
  - **behavior:** represents the behavior (functionality) of an object such as deposit, withdraw etc.
  - **identity:** Object identity is typically implemented via a unique ID. The value of the ID is not visible to the external user. But,it is used internally by the JVM to identify each object uniquely.
- For Example: Pen is an object. Its name is Reynolds, color is white etc. known as its state. It is used to write, so writing is its behavior.
- Object is an instance of a class. Class is a template or blueprint from which objects are created. So object is the instance(result) of a class.

### *Creating an Object*

As mentioned previously, a class provides the blueprints for objects. So basically an object is created from a class. In Java, the new key word is used to create new objects.

There are three steps when creating an object from a class:

- **Declaration:** A variable declaration with a variable name with an object type.
- **Instantiation:** The 'new' key word is used to create the object.
- **Initialization:** The 'new' keyword is followed by a call to a constructor. This call initializes the new object.
- To create object of a class ***<new> Keyword*** can be used.

***Syntax***

***<Class_Name> ClassObjectReference = new <Class_Name>();***

Here constructor of the class(*Class_Name*) will get executed and object will be created(ClassObjectRefrence *will hold the reference of created object in memory*).

**The new() operator**

Using Person class, you can create any number of objects using new() operator.The syntax is

**classname objectname = new classname();**

When a reference is made to a particular student with its property then it becomes an **object**, physical existence of Student class.

***Student std=new Student();***

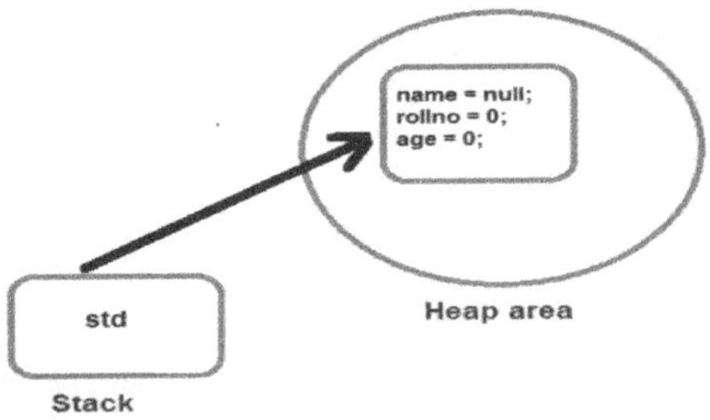


After the above statement std is instance/object of Student class. Here the new keyword creates an actual physical copy of the object and assign it to the std variable. It will have physical existence and get memory in heap area. The new operator dynamically allocates memory for an object.

*Simple Example of Object and Class*

In this example, we have created a Student class that have two data members id and name. We are creating the object of the Student class by new keyword and printing the objects value.

```
class Student1{
 int id=100;//data member (also instance variable)
int marks=500 ;//data member(also instance variable)
  public static void main(String args[]){
 Student1 s1=new Student1();//creating an object of Student
 System.out.println(s1.id);
 System.out.println(s1.marks);
 }
}
```

*OutPut*

```
E:\JAVA>javac Student1.java
E:\JAVA>java Student1
100
500
```

## 2.15. Methods in Java

- Method describe behavior of an object. A method is a collection of statements that are group together to perform an operation.
- A method is like function i.e. used to expose behavior of an object.
- Advantage of Method
    - Code Reusability
    - Code Optimization

*Syntax*

```
return-type methodName(parameter-list)
{
 //body of method
}
```

*Example of a Method*

```
public String getName(String st)
{
```

```
String name="StudyTonight";
name=name+st;
return name;
}
```

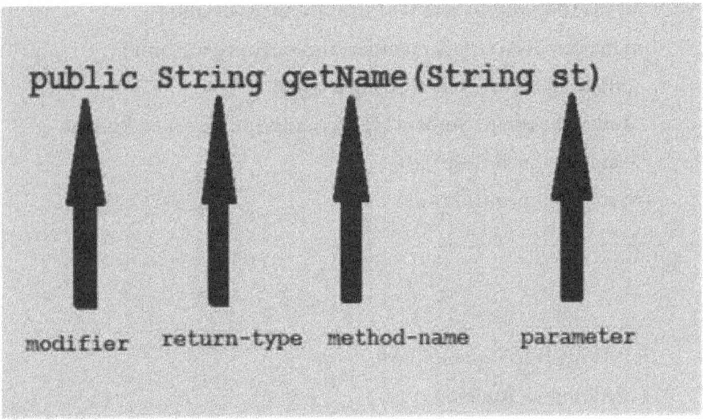


**Modifier:** Modifier are access type of method. We will discuss it in detail later.

**Return Type :** A method may return value. Data type of value return by a method is declare in method heading.

**Method name :** Actual name of the method.

**Parameter :** Value passed to a method.

**Method body :** collection of statement that defines what method does.

- Methods define actions that a class's objects (or instances) can do.
- A method has a declaration part and a body.
- The declaration part consists of a return value, the method name, and a list of arguments.
- The body contains code that perform the action.
- The return type of a method can be a primitive, an object, or void.
- The return type void means that the method returns nothing.
- The declaration part of a method is also called the signature of the method.

***Example***

```
public class MethodExample{
public static void PrintLine() {
```

```
System.out.println("This is a line of text.");
}
public static void main(String[] args) {
System.out.println("Start Here");
PrintLine();
System.out.println("Back to the Main");
PrintLine();
System.out.println("End Here");
}
}
```

*OutPut*

```
E:\JAVA>javac MethodExample.java
E:\JAVA>java MethodExample
Start Here
This is a line of text.
Back to the Main
This is a line of text.
End Here
```

*Example: Method with Arguments*

```
class Method
{
public static void main(String args[])
  {
     Method obj = new Method();
     obj.disp('a');
     obj.disp('a',10);
  }
   public void disp(char c)
   {
      System.out.println(c);
   }
   public void disp(char c, int num)
   {
```

```
            System.out.println(c + " "+num);
        }
    }
```

***OutPut***

```
E:\JAVA>javac Method.java
E:\JAVA>java Method
a
a 10
```

## *Access Control*

- Java provides control over the visibility of variables and methods.
- Encapsulation, safely sealing data within the capsule of the class Prevents programmers from relying on details of class implementation, so you can update without worry
- Helps in protecting against accidental or wrong usage.
- Keeps code elegant and clean (easier to maintain)

## *Access Modifiers*

a. Public

b. Private

c. Protected

d. Default

- Access modifiers help you set the level of access you want for your class, variables as well as methods.
- Access modifiers (Some or All) can be applied on Class, Variable, Methods

## *Java Access Modifiers Table for Class*

| Visibility | Public Access Modifier | Default Access Modifier |
|---|---|---|
| Within Same Package | Yes | Yes |
| From Outside the Same Package | Yes | No |

### *Public*

When set to public, the given class will be accessible to all the classes available in Java world.

### *Default*

When set to default, the given class will be accessible to the classes which are defined in the same package.

### *Access Modifiers for Variable (Instance / Static Variable)*

- Default
- Public
- Protected
- Private

**Note*:** Visibility of the class should be checked before checking the visibility of the variable defined inside that class. If the class is visible only then the variables defined inside that class will be visible. If the class is not visible then no variable will be accessible, even if it is set to public.

### *Default*

If a variable is set to default, it will be accessible to the classes which are defined in the same package. Any method in any class which is defined in the same package can access the variable *via* ***Inheritance*** *or* ***Direct access.***

### *Public*

If a variable is set to public it can be accessible from any class available in the Java world. Any method in any class can access the given variable *via* ***Inheritance*** *or* ***Direct access.***

### *Protected*

If a variable is set to protected inside a class, it will be accessible from its sub classes defined in the same or different package only via ***Inheritance***.

**Note:** The only difference between protected and default is that protected access modifiers respect **class subclass relation** while default does not.

### *Private*

A variable if defined private will be accessible only from within the class it is defined. Such variables are not accessible from outside the defined class, not even its subclass.

Java Access Modifiers Table for Variable.

| **Visibility** | **Public Access Modifier** | **Private Access Modifier** | **Protected Access Modifier** | **Default Access Modifier** |
|---|---|---|---|---|
| Within Same Class | Yes | Yes | Yes | Yes |
| From Any Class in Same Package | Yes | No | Yes | Yes |
| From Any Sub Class in Same Package | Yes | No | Yes | Yes |
| From Any Sub Class from Different Package | Yes | No | Yes(**Only By Inheritance**) | No |
| From Any Non Sub Class in Different Package | Yes | No | No | No |

### *Access Modifiers for Methods*

Methods are eligible for all of the above mentioned modifiers.

### *Default*

When a method is set to default it will be accessible to the class which are defined in the same package. Any method in any class which is defined in the same package can access the given method *via* ***Inheritance*** *or* ***Direct access***.

### *Public*

When a method is set to public it will be accessible from any class available in the Java world. Any method in any class can access the given method via ***Inheritance*** *or* ***Direct access*** depending on class level access.

### *Protected*

If a method is set to protected inside a class, it will be accessible from its sub classes defined in the same or different package.

**Note:*** The only difference between protected and default is that protected access modifiers respect **class subclass relation** while default does not.

### *Private*

A method if defined private will be accessible only from within the class it is defined. Such methods are not accessible from outside the defined class, not even its subclass.

Java Access Modifiers Table for Method.

| **Visibility** | **Public Access Modifier** | **Private Access Modifier** | **Protected Access Modifier** | **Default Access Modifier** |
|---|---|---|---|---|
| Within Same Class | Yes | Yes | Yes | Yes |
| From Any Class in Same Package | Yes | No | Yes | Yes |
| From Any Sub Class in Same Package | Yes | No | Yes | Yes |
| From Any Sub Class from Different Package | Yes | No | Yes(**Only By Inheritance**) | No |
| From Any Non Sub Class in Different Package | Yes | No | No | No |

## 2.16. Constructors

A constructor is a special member method which will be called by the JVM implicitly (automatically) for placing user/programmer defined values instead of placing default values. Constructors are meant for initializing the object.

### *Advantages of Constructors*

- A constructor eliminates placing the default values.
- A constructor eliminates calling the normal method implicitly.

### *Rules/Properties/Characteristics of a Constructor*

- Constructor name must be similar to name of the class.
- Constructor should not return any value even void also (if we write the return type for the constructor then that constructor will be treated as ordinary method).

- Constructors should not be static since constructors will be called each and every time whenever an object is creating.
- Constructor should not be private provided an object of one class is created in another class (constructor can be private provided an object of one class created in the same class).
- Constructors will not be inherited at all.
- Constructors are called automatically whenever an object is creating.

### *Types of Constructors*

Based on creating objects in JAVA we have two types of constructors.

They are

- Default/parameter less/no argument constructor.
- Parameterized constructor.

A default constructor is one which will not take any parameters.

### *Syntax*

```
class <clsname>
{
clsname () //default constructor
{
Block of statements;
.................................;
.................................;
}
..........................;
..........................;
};
```

### *For example*

```
class Test
{
int a, b;
```

```
Test ()
{
    System.out.println ("I AM FROM DEFAULT CONSTRUCTOR...");
    a=10;
    b=20;
    System.out.println ("VALUE OF a = "+a);
    System.out.println ("VALUE OF b = "+b);
}
}
class TestDemo
{
public static void main (String [] args)
{
    Test t1=new Test ();
}
}
```

***OutPut***

```
E:\JAVA>javac TestDemo.java
E:\JAVA>java TestDemo
I AM FROM DEFAULT CONSTRUCTOR...
VALUE OF a = 10
VALUE OF b = 20
```

***RULE-1***

Whenever we create an object only with default constructor, defining the default constructor is optional. If we are not defining default constructor of a class, then JVM will call automatically system defined default constructor (SDDC). If we define, JVM will call user/programmer defined default constructor (UDDC).

A Parameterized Constructor is one which takes some parameters.

***Syntax***

```
class <clsname>
{
..............................;
```

```
..............................;
<clsname> (list of parameters) //parameterized constructor
{
Block of statements (s);
}
..............................;
..............................;
}
```

*For example*

```
class Test
{
int a, b;
Test (int n1, int n2)
{
System.out.println ("I AM FROM PARAMETER CONSTRUCTOR...");
a=n1;
b=n2;
System.out.println ("VALUE OF a = "+a);
System.out.println ("VALUE OF b = "+b);
}
}
class TestDemo1
{
public static void main (String k [])
{
Test t1=new Test (10, 20);
}
}
```

*OutPut*

```
E:\JAVA>javac TestDemo1.java
E:\JAVA>java TestDemo1
```

*I AM FROM PARAMETER CONSTRUCTOR...*

*VALUE OF a = 10*

*VALUE OF b = 20*

***RULE-2***

- Whenever we create an object using parameterized constructor, it is mandatory for the JAVA programmer to define parameterized constructor otherwise we will get compile time error.

## 2.17. Constructor Overloaded

Overloaded constructor is one in which constructor name is similar but its signature is different.

Signature represents number of parameters, type of parameters and order of parameters. Here, at least one thing must be differentiated.

***For Example***

```
Test t1=new Test (10, 20);
Test t2=new Test (10, 20, 30);
Test t3=new Test (10.5, 20.5);
Test t4=new Test (10, 20.5);
Test t5=new Test (10.5, 20);
```

***RULE-3***

Whenever we define/create the objects with respect to both parameterized constructor and default constructor, it is mandatory for the JAVA programmer to define both the constructors.

***NOTE***

When we define a class, that class can contain two categories of constructors they are single default constructor and 'n' number of parameterized constructors (overloaded constructors).

***Example***

```
class Test
{
int a, b;
```

```
Test ()
{
    System.out.println ("I AM FROM DEFAULT CONSTRUCTOR...");
    a=1;
    b=2;
    System.out.println ("VALUE OF a ="+a);
    System.out.println ("VALUE OF b ="+b);
}
Test (int x, int y)
{
    System.out.println ("I AM FROM DOUBLE PARAMETERIZED
CONSTRUCTOR...");
    a=x;
    b=y;
    System.out.println ("VALUE OF a ="+a);
    System.out.println ("VALUE OF b ="+b);
}
Test (int x)
{
    System.out.println ("I AM FROM SINGLE PARAMETERIZED
CONSTRUCTOR...");
    a=x;
    b=x;
    System.out.println ("VALUE OF a ="+a);
    System.out.println ("VALUE OF b ="+b);
}
Test (Test T)
{
    System.out.println ("I AM FROM OBJECT PARAMETERIZED
CONSTRUCTOR...");
    a=T.a;
    b=T.b;
    System.out.println ("VALUE OF a ="+a);
    System.out.println ("VALUE OF b ="+b);
```

```
}
}
class TestDemo2
{
public static void main (String k [])
{
    Test t1=new Test ();
    Test t2=new Test (10, 20);
    Test t3=new Test (1000);
    Test t4=new Test (t1);
}
}
```

***Output***

```
E:\JAVA>javac TestDemo2.java
E:\JAVA>java TestDemo2
I AM FROM DEFAULT CONSTRUCTOR...
VALUE OF a =1
VALUE OF b =2
I AM FROM DOUBLE PARAMETERIZED CONSTRUCTOR...
VALUE OF a =10
VALUE OF b =20
I AM FROM SINGLE PARAMETERIZED CONSTRUCTOR...
VALUE OF a =1000
VALUE OF b =1000
I AM FROM OBJECT PARAMETERIZED CONSTRUCTOR...
VALUE OF a =1
VALUE OF b =2
```

## 2.18. 'this'

In java, this is a reference variable that refers to the current object.

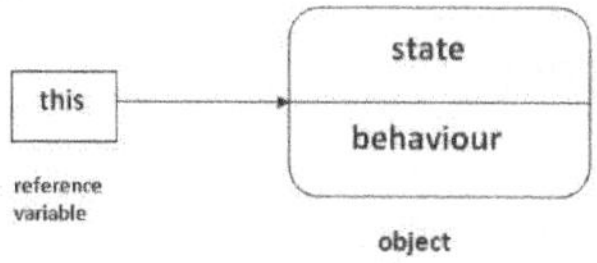

- 'this' is an internal or implicit object created by JAVA for two purposes. They are
- 'this' object is internally pointing to current class object.
- Whenever the formal parameters and data members of the class are similar, to differentiate the data members of the class from formal parameters, the data members of class must be proceeded by 'this'.
- this (): this () is used for calling current class default constructor from current class parameterized constructors.
- this (...): this (...) is used for calling current class parameterized constructor from other category constructors of the same class.

### *Usage of Java this Keyword*

1. The this keyword can be used to refer current class instance variable.
2. this() can be used to invoked current class constructor.

### *Rule for 'this'*

- Whenever we use either this () or this (...) in the current class constructors, that statements must be used as first statement only.
- The order of the output containing this () or this (...) will be in the reverse order of the input which we gave as inputs.

### *NOTE*

Whenever we refer the data members which are similar to formal parameters, the JVM gives first preference to formal parameters whereas whenever we write a keyword this before the variable name of a class then the JVM refers to data members of the class. this methods are used for calling current class constructors.

### *NOTE*

- If any method called by an object then that object is known as source object.
- If we pass an object as a parameter to the method then that object is known as target object.

### *Examples*

**1) The this keyword can be used to refer current class instance variable.**

```
class Student{
   int id;
   int marks;
```

```
Student(int id, int marks){
this.id = id;
this.marks = marks;
}
void display(){System.out.println(id+" "+marks);}
public static void main(String args[]){ Student s1 =
new Student(111,1500);
Student s2 = new Student(222,2000);
s1.display();
s2.display();
}
}
```

*Out Put*

```
E:\JAVA>javac Student.java
E:\JAVA>java Student
111 1500
222 2000
```

2) this() can be used to invoked current class constructor.

```
class Student{
int id
int marks;
Student()
{
System.out.println("default constructor is invoked");
}
Student(int id, int marks){
this();
this.id = id;
this.marks = marks;
}
void display()
{
System.out.println(id+" "+marks);
}
```

```
public static void main(String args[])
{
 Student s1 = new Student(111,1500);
Student s2 = new Student(222,2000);
s1.display();
s2.display();}
}
```

*OutPut*

```
E:\JAVA>javac Student.java
E:\JAVA>java Student
default constructor is invoked
default constructor is invoked
111  1500
222  2000
```

## 2.19. Java Static Keyword

The **static keyword** in java is used for memory management mainly. We can apply java static keyword with variables, methods, blocks and nested class.

The static keyword belongs to the class than instance of the class.

The static can be:

1. variable (also known as class variable)
2. method (also known as class method)

### *1) Java Static Variable*

If you declare any variable as static, it is known static variable.

- The static variable can be used to refer the common property of all objects (that is not unique for each object) e.g. company name of employees, college name of students etc.
- The static variable gets memory only once in class area at the time of class loading.

### *Advantage of Static Variable*

- It makes your program **memory efficient** (i.e it saves memory).

### *Understanding Problem without Static Variable*

```
class Student{
   int rollno;
```

```
        String name;
        String college="PACE";
    }
```

Suppose there are 500 students in my college, now all instance data members will get memory each time when object is created. All student have its unique rollno and name so instance data member is good. Here, college refers to the common property of all objects.If we make it static, this field will get memory only once.

### *Example of Static Variable*

```
class Student8{
  int rollno;
  String name;
  static String college ="PACE";
  Student8(int r,String n){
  rollno = r;
  name = n;
  }
 void display (){
   System.out.println(rollno+" "+name+" "+college);
 }
 public static void main(String args[]){
     Student8 s1 = new Student8(111,"Karan");
     Student8 s2 = new Student8(222,"Aryan");
     s1.display();
     s2.display();
 }
}
```

***Output: 111 Karan PACE***

***222 Aryan PACE***

### *2) Java Static Method*

If you apply static keyword with any method, it is known as static method.

- A static method belongs to the class rather than object of a class.
- A static method can be invoked without the need for creating an instance of a class.
- Static method can access static data member and can change the value of it.

### *Example of Static Method*

```
class Student9{
   int rollno;
   String name;
   static String college = "PACE";
   static void change(){
   college = "VELS";
   }
    Student9(int r, String n){
   rollno = r;
   name = n;
   }
    void display ()
    {
         System.out.println(rollno+" "+name+" "+college);
    }
     public static void main(String args[]){
         Student9.change();
         Student9 s1 = new Student9 (111,"Karan");
         Student9 s2 = new Student9 (222,"Aryan");
         Student9 s3 = new Student9 (333,"Sonoo");
         s1.display();
         s2.display();
         s3.display();
   }
}
Output:111 Karan VELS
       222 Aryan VELS
       333 Sonoo VELS
```

### *Restrictions for Static Method*

There are two main restrictions for the static method. They are:

- The static method can not use non static data member or call non-static method directly.

This cannot be used in static context.

## 2.20. Arrays

Arrays are generally effective means of storing groups of variables. An array is a group of variables that share the same name and are ordered sequentially from zero to one less than the number of variables in the array.

The number of variables that can be stored in an array is called the array's dimension. Each variable in the array is called an element of the array.

### *Creating Arrays*

There are three steps to creating an array, declaring it, allocating it and initializing it.

### *Declaring Arrays*

Like other variables in Java, an array must have a specific type like byte, int, String or double. Only variables of the appropriate type can be stored in an array.

You cannot have an array that will store both ints and Strings, for instance.

Like all other variables in Java an array must be declared. When you declare an array variable you suffix the type with [] to indicate that this variable is an array. Here are some examples:

```
int[] k;
float[] yt;
String[] names;
```

In other words you declare an array like you'd declare any other variable except you append brackets to the end of the variable type.

### *Allocating Arrays*

Declaring an array merely says what it is. It does not create the array. To actually create the array (or any other object) use the new operator.

When we create an array we need to tell the compiler how many elements will be stored in it. Here's how we'd create the variables declared above: new

```
k = new int[3];
yt = new float[7];
names = new String[50];
```

The numbers in the brackets specify the dimension of the array; i.e. how many slots it has to hold values. With the dimensions above k can hold three ints, yt can hold seven floats and names can hold fifty Strings.

## *Initializing Arrays*

Individual elements of the array are referenced by the array name and by an integer which represents their position in the array. The numbers we use to identify them are called subscripts or indexes into the array. Subscripts are consecutive integers beginning with 0. Thus the array k above has elements k[0], k[1], and k[2]. Since we started counting at zero there is no k[3], and trying to access it will generate an ArrayIndexOutOfBoundsException. subscripts indexes k k[0] k[1] k[2] k[3]

**ArrayIndexOutOfBoundsException**

You can use array elements wherever you'd use a similarly typed variable that wasn't part of an array.

Here's how we'd store values in the arrays we've been working with:

```
k[0] = 2;
k[1] = 5;
k[2] = -2;
yt[6] = 7.5f;
names[4] = "Fred";
```

This step is called initializing the array or, more precisely, initializing the elements of the array. Sometimes the phrase "initializing the array" would be reserved for when we initialize all the elements of the array. For even medium sized arrays, it's unwieldy to specify each element individually. It is often helpful to use for loops to initialize the array. For instance here is a loop that fills an array with the squares of the numbers from 0 to 100.

```
float[] squares = new float[101];
for (int i=0; i <= 500; i++) {
  squares[i] = i*2;
}
```

## *Two Dimensional Arrays*

Two dimensional arrays are declared, allocated and initialized much like one dimensional arrays. However we have to specify two dimensions rather than one, and we typically use two nested for loops to fill the array. for The array examples above are filled with the sum of their row and column indices. Here's some code that would create and fill such an array:

```
class FillArray {
  public static void main (String args[]) {
```

```
int[][] M;
M = new int[4][5];
for (int row=0; row < 4; row++) {
  for (int col=0; col < 5; col++) {
    M[row][col] = row+col;
  }
}
}
}
```

In two-dimensional arrays ArrayIndexOutOfBounds errors occur whenever you exceed the maximum column index or row index. Unlike two-dimensional C arrays, two-dimensional Java arrays are not just one-dimensional arrays indexed in a funny way.

### *Multidimensional Arrays*

You don't have to stop with two dimensional arrays. Java lets you have arrays of three, four or more dimensions.

However chances are pretty good that if you need more than three dimensions in an array, you're probably using the wrong data structure. Even three dimensional arrays are exceptionally rare outside of scientific and engineering applications.

The syntax for three dimensional arrays is a direct extension of that for two-dimensional arrays. Here's a program that declares, allocates and initializes a three-dimensional array:

```
class Fill3DArray {
 public static void main (String args[]) {
  int[][][] M;
  M = new int[4][5][3];
  for (int row=0; row < 4; row++) {
    for (int col=0; col < 5; col++) {
      for (int ver=0; ver < 3; ver++) {
        M[row][col][ver] = row+col+ver;
      }
    }
  }
 }
}
```

### *Strings*

- Strings, which are widely used in Java programming, are a sequence of characters. In the Java programming language, strings are objects.
- The Java platform provides the String class to create and manipulate strings.

### *Creating Strings*

The most direct way to create a string is to write:

***String greeting = "Hello world!";***

In this case, "Hello world!" is a string literal—a series of characters in your code that is enclosed in double quotes.

Whenever it encounters a string literal in your code, the compiler creates a String object with its value—in this case, Hello world!.

As with any other object, you can create String objects by using the new keyword and a constructor.

The String class has thirteen constructors that allow you to provide the initial value of the string using different sources, such as an array of characters:

```
char[] helloArray = { 'h', 'e', 'l', 'l', 'o',
'.'}; String helloString = new
String(helloArray);
System.out.println(helloString);
```

The last line of this code snippet displays hello.

### *String Length*

Methods used to obtain information about an object are known as accessor methods. One accessor method that you can use with strings is the length() method, which returns the number of characters contained in the string object. After the following two lines of code have been executed, len equals 17:

```
String palindrome = "Dot saw I was Tod";
int len = palindrome.length();
```

A palindrome is a word or sentence that is symmetric—it is spelled the same forward and backward, ignoring case and punctuation.

Here is a short and inefficient program to reverse a palindrome string. It invokes the String method charAt(i), which returns the ith character in the string, counting from 0.

```
public class StringDemo {
   public static void main(String[] args)
     {
            String palindrome = "Dot saw I was Tod";
            int len =
     palindrome.length();
            char[] tempCharArray = new char[len];
            char[] charArray = new char[len];
            //put original string in an array of chars
        for (int i = 0; i < len; i++) {
            tempCharArray[i] = palindrome.charAt(i);
        }
     // reverse array of chars
       for (int j = 0; j < len; j++) {
            charArray[j] = tempCharArray[len - 1 - j];
       }
       String reversePalindrome = new String(charArray);
     System.out.println(reversePalindrome);
   }
   }
```

### *Running the Program Produces this Output*

**doT saw I was toD**

To accomplish the string reversal, the program had to convert the string to an array of characters (first for loop), reverse the array into a second array (second for loop), and then convert back to a string. The String class includes a method, getChars(), to convert a string, or a portion of a string, into an array of characters so we could replace the first for loop in the program above with palindrome.getChars(0, len, tempCharArray, 0);

### *Concatenating Strings*

The String class includes a method for concatenating two strings:

**string1.concat(string2);**

This returns a new string that is string1 with string2 added to it at the end.

You can also use the concat() method with string literals, as in:

"My name is ".concat("Rumplestiltskin");

Strings are more commonly concatenated with the + operator, as in

"Hello," + " world" + "!"

which results in

"Hello, world!"

The + operator is widely used in print statements. For example:

String string1 = "saw I was ";

System.out.println("Dot " + string1 + "Tod");

which prints

Dot saw I was Tod

## 2.21. Java Command Line Arguments

- The java command-line argument is an argument i.e. passed at the time of running the java program.
- The arguments passed from the console can be received in the java program and it can be used as an input.
- So, it provides a convenient way to check the behavior of the program for the different values. You can pass N (1,2,3 and so on) numbers of arguments from the command prompt.

### *Simple Example of Command-line Argument in Java*

In this example, we are receiving only one argument and printing it. To run this java program, you must pass at least one argument from the command prompt.

```
class CommandLineExample{
public static void main(String args[]){
    System.out.println("Your first argument is: "+args[0]);
}
}
```

***OutPut***

```
D:\>javac CommandLineExample.java
D:\>java CommandLineExample PACE
Your first argument is: PACE
```

### *Example of Command-line Argument That Prints All the Values*

In this example, we are printing all the arguments passed from the command-line.

For this purpose, we have traversed the array using for loop.

```
class A{
public static void main(String args[]){
for(int i=0;i<args.length;i++)
System.out.println(args[i]);
 }
}
```

### *OutPut*

```
D:\>javac A.java
D:\>java A 1 2 3 PACE Cse
1
2
3
PACE
Cse
```

# CHAPTER III

# Inheritance

## 3.1. Inheritance in Java

**Inheritance in java** is a mechanism in which one object acquires all the properties and behaviours of parent object.

The idea behind inheritance in java is that you can create new classes that are built upon existing classes. When you inherit from an existing class, you can reuse methods and fields of parent class, and you can add new methods and fields also.

Inheritance represents the **IS-A relationship**, also known as ***parent-child*** relationship.

Syntax of Java Inheritance

```
class Subclass-name extends Superclass-name
{
  //methods and fields
}
```

The **extends keyword** indicates that you are making a new class that derives from an existing class.

In the terminology of Java, a class that is inherited is called a super class. The new class is called a subclass.

### *Types of Inheritance in Java*

On the basis of class, there can be three types of inheritance in java: single, multilevel and hierarchical.

In java programming, multiple and hybrid inheritance is supported through **interface** only.

When a class extends multiple classes i.e. known as multiple inheritance.

#### *a) Why Multiple Inheritance is not Supported in Java?*

To reduce the complexity and simplify the language, multiple inheritance is not supported in java.

Consider a scenario where A, B and C are three classes. The C class inherits A and B classes.

If A and B classes have same method and you call it from child class object, there will be ambiguity to call method of A or B class.

Since compile time errors are better than runtime errors, java renders compile time error if you inherit 2 classes. So whether you have same method or different, there will be compile time error now.

```
class A{
    void msg(){System.out.println("Hello");}
}
class B{
    void msg(){System.out.println("Welcome");}
}
class C extends A,B{//suppose if it were
     Public Static void main(String args[]){
         C obj=new C();
         obj.msg();//Now which msg() method would be invoked?
     }
}
```

***Output***

Compile Time Error.

## 3.2. Method Overloading

If a class have multiple methods by same name but different parameters, it is known as **Method Overloading**.

If we have to perform only one operation, having same name of the methods increases the readability of the program.

### *Advantage of Method Overloading?*

Method Overloading **increases the readability of the program**.

### *Different Ways to Overload the Method*

There are two ways to overload the method in java:

1. By changing number of arguments
2. By changing the data type

***In java, Method Overloading is not possible by changing the return type of the method.***

## 3.3. Super Keyword

The **super** keyword in java is a reference variable that is used to refer immediate parent class object.

Whenever you create the instance of subclass, an instance of parent class is created implicitly i.e. referred by super reference variable.

### *Usage of Java Super Keyword*

1. super is used to refer immediate parent class instance variable.
2. super() is used to invoke immediate parent class constructor.
3. super is used to invoke immediate parent class method.

## 3.4. Final Keyword

The **final keyword** in java is used to restrict the user. The java final keyword can be used in many contexts. Final can be:

1. variable
2. method
3. class

The final keyword can be applied with the variables, a final variable that have no value it is called blank final variable or uninitialized final variable.

It can be initialized in the constructor only. The blank final variable can be static also which will be initialized in the static block only.

### *1) Final Variable*

If you make any variable as final, you cannot change the value of final variable(It will be constant).

### *2) Final Method*

If you make any method as final, you cannot override it.

### *3) Final Class*

If you make any class as final, you cannot extend it.

## 3.5. Abstract Class in Java

A class that is declared with abstract keyword, is known as abstract class in java. It can have abstract and non-abstract methods (method with body).

A class that is declared as abstract is known as **abstract class**. It needs to be extended and its method implemented. It cannot be instantiated.

### *Example Abstract Class*

```
abstract class A {}
```

### *Abstract Method*

A method that is declared as abstract and does not have implementation is known as abstract method.

### *Example Abstract Method*

```
abstract void printStatus();//no body and abstract
```

### *Example of Abstract Class that has Abstract Method*

In this example, Bike the abstract class that contains only one abstract method run. It implementation is provided by the Honda class.

```
abstract class Bike
{
    abstract void run();
}
class Honda4 extends Bike{
    void run()
    {
        System.out.println("running safely..");
    }
    public static void main(String args[])
    {
        Bike obj = new Honda4();
        obj.run();
    }
}
```

### *Output*

running safely.

### *Another Example of Abstract Class in Java*

*File: TestBank.java*

```
abstract class Bank
{
        abstract int getRateOfInterest();
}
class SBI extends Bank
{
        int getRateOfInterest(){return 7;}
}
class PNB extends Bank{
        int getRateOfInterest()
        {
            return 7;
        }
}
class TestBank{
        public static void main(String args[])
        {
            Bank b=new SBI();//if object is PNB, method of PNB will be invoked
            int interest=b.getRateOfInterest();
            System.out.println("Rate of Interest is: "+interest+" %");
        }
}
```

### *Output*

```
Rate of Interest is: 7 %
```

## 3.6. Interface in Java

An **interface in java** is a blueprint of a class. It has static constants and abstract methods only.

The interface in java is **a mechanism to achieve fully abstraction**. There can be only abstract methods in the java interface not method body. It is used to achieve fully abstraction and multiple inheritances in Java.

Java Interface also **represents IS-A relationship**.

It cannot be instantiated just like abstract class.

### *Why Use Java Interface?*

There are mainly three reasons to use interface. They are given below.

- It is used to achieve fully abstraction.
- By interface, we can support the functionality of multiple inheritance.

**NOTE: Interface fields are public, static and final by default, and methods are public and abstract.**

Understanding relationship between classes and interfaces

As shown in the figure given below, a class extends another class, an interface extends another interface but a class implements an interface.

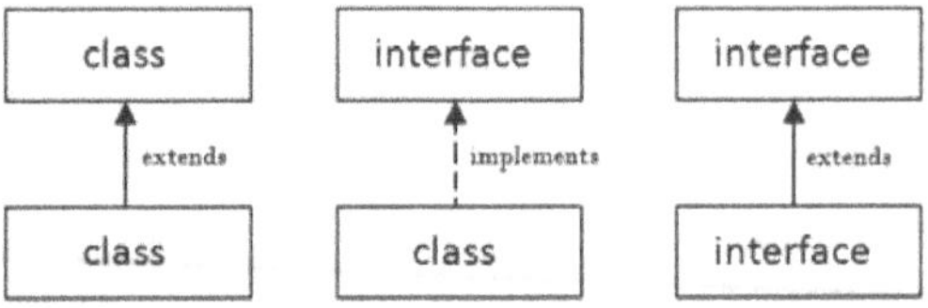


### *Simple Example of Java Interface*

In this example, Printable interface have only one method, its implementation is provided in the A class.

```
interface printable {
void print();
}
class A6 implements printable {
public void print()
{System.out.println("Hello");
}
public static void main(String args[]){
A6 obj = new A6();
obj.print();
 }
}
```

***Output***

Output: Hello

*Multiple inheritances in Java by interface*

If a class implements multiple interfaces, or an interface extends multiple interfaces i.e. known as multiple inheritance.

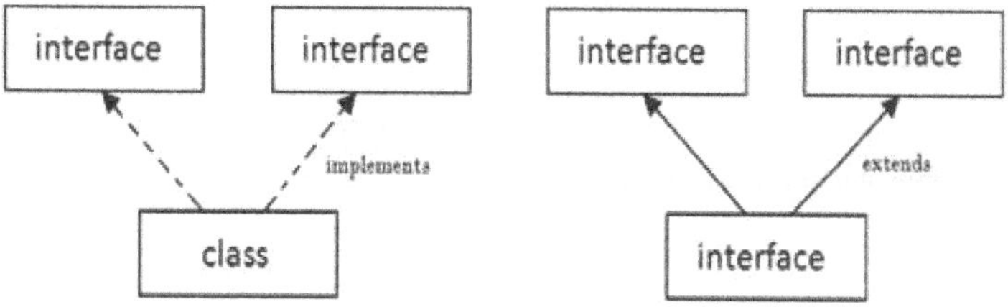


**Multiple Inheritance in Java**

```
interface Printable{
void print();
}
interface Showable{
void show();
}
class A7 implements Printable,Showable{
public void print(){System.out.println("Hello");}
public void show(){System.out.println("Welcome");}
public static void main(String args[]){
A7 obj = new A7();
obj.print();
obj.show();
 }
}
```

***Output***

Output: Hello
Welcome

*Q) What is marker or tagged interface?*

An interface that have no member is known as marker or tagged interface. For example: Serializable, Cloneable, Remote etc. They are used to provide some essential information to the JVM so that JVM may perform some useful operation.

```
//How Serializable interface is written?
public interface Serializable
{
}
```

**Nested Interface in Java**

**An interface can have another interface i.e. known as nested interface. We will learn it in detail in the nested classes chapter.**

***For Example***

```
interface printable{
    void print();
interface MessagePrintable
{
     void msg();
}
}
```

## 3.7. Java Package

A **java package** is a group of similar types of classes, interfaces and sub-packages.

Package in java can be categorized in two form, built-in package and user-defined package. There are many built-in packages such as java, lang, awt, javax, swing, net, io, util, sql etc.

Here, we will have the detailed learning of creating and using user-defined packages.

### *Advantage of Java Package*

1. Java package is used to categorize the classes and interfaces so that they can be easily maintained.
2. Java package provides access protection.
3. Java package removes naming collision.

### *Simple Example of Java Package*

The **package keyword** is used to create a package in java.

```
//save as Simple.java
```

```
package mypack;
public class Simple{
  public static void main(String args[]){
     System.out.println("Welcome to package");
  }
}
```

### *How to Compile Java Package*

If you are not using any IDE, you need to follow the **syntax** given below:

javac -d directory javafilename

### *For Example*

javac -d . Simple.java

The -d switch specifies the destination where to put the generated class file.

### *How to Run Java Package Program*

You need to use fully qualified name e.g. mypack.Simple etc to run the class.

**To Compile:** javac -d . Simple.java

**To Run:** java mypack.Simple

Output: Welcome to package

The -d is a switch that tells the compiler where to put the class file i.e. it represents destination. The . Represents the current folder.

### *How to Access Package from Another Package?*

There are three ways to access the package from outside the package.

1. Import package.*;
2. Import package.classname;
3. Fully qualified name.
4. Using packagename.*

If you use package.* then all the classes and interfaces of this package will be accessible but not subpackages.

The import keyword is used to make the classes and interface of another package accessible to the current package

### *1) Example of Package that Import the Packagename.**

```
//save by A.java
package pack;
public class A{
        public void msg(){System.out.println("Hello");}
}
//save by B.java
package mypack;
import pack.*;
class B{
public static void main(String args[]){
    A obj = new A();
    obj.msg();
 }
}
Output: Hello
```

### *2) Using packagename.classname*

If you import package.classname then only declared class of this package will be accessible.

*Example of package by import package.classname*

```
//save by A.java
package pack;
public class A{
        public void msg()
        {
           System.out.println("Hello");
        }
}
//save by B.java
package mypack;
import pack.A;
class B{
public static void main(String args[]){
A obj = new A();
```

```
obj.msg();
}
}
```

Output: Hello

### *3) Using fully qualified name*

If you use fully qualified name then only declared class of this package will be accessible. Now there is no need to import. But you need to use fully qualified name every time when you are accessing the class or interface.

It is generally used when two packages have same class name e.g. java.util and java.sql packages contain Date class.

*Example of package by import fully qualified name*

```
//save by A.java
    package pack;
    public class A{
        public void msg(){System.out.println("Hello");}
    }
    //save by B.java
    package mypack;
    class B{
        public static void main(String args[]){
                pack.A obj = new pack.A();//using fully qualified name
                obj.msg();
            }
    }
```

Output: Hello

## 3.8. Exception Handling

The **exception handling in java** is one of the powerful *mechanism to handle the runtime errors* so that normal flow of the application can be maintained.

**What is exception**

**Dictionary Meaning:** Exception is an abnormal condition.

In java, exception is an event that disrupts the normal flow of the program. It is an object which is thrown at runtime.

What is exception handling.

Exception Handling is a mechanism to handle runtime errors such as ClassNotFound, IO, SQL, Remote etc.

### *Advantage of Exception Handling*

**The core advantage of exception handling is** to maintain the normal flow of the application.

**Exception normally disrupts the normal flow of the application that is why we use exception handling.**

Let's take a scenario:

```
statement 1;
statement 2;
statement 3;
statement 4;
statement 5;//exception occurs
statement 6;
statement 7;
statement 8;
statement 9;
statement 10;
```

Suppose there is 10 statements in your program and there occurs an exception at statement 5, rest of the code will not be executed i.e. statement 6 to 10 will not run. If we perform exception handling, rest of the exception will be executed. That is why we use exception handling in java.

### *Types of Exception*

There are mainly two types of exceptions: checked and unchecked where error is considered as unchecked exception. The sun microsystem says there are three types of exceptions:

1. Checked Exception
2. Unchecked Exception
3. Error

### *Difference between Checked and Unchecked Exceptions*

### *1) Checked Exception*

The classes that extend Throwable class except RuntimeException and Error are known as checked exceptions e.g. IOException, SQLException etc. Checked exceptions are checked at compile-time.

### *2) Unchecked Exception*

The classes that extend RuntimeException are known as unchecked exceptions e.g.

ArithmeticException, NullPointerException, ArrayIndexOutOfBoundsException etc.

Unchecked exceptions are not checked at compile-time rather they are checked at runtime.

### *3) Error*

Error is irrecoverable e.g. OutOfMemoryError, VirtualMachineError, AssertionError etc.

### *Common Scenarios Where Exceptions may Occur*

There are given some scenarios where unchecked exceptions can occur. They are as follows:

### *1) Scenario where Arithmetic Exception Occurs*

If we divide any number by zero, there occurs an ArithmeticException.

```
int a=50/0;//ArithmeticException
```

### *2) Scenario where Null Pointer Exception occurs*

If we have null value in any variable, performing any operation by the variable occurs an NullPointerException.

```
String s=null;
System.out.println(s.length());//NullPointerException
```

### *3) Scenario where Number Format Exception occurs*

The wrong formatting of any value, may occur NumberFormatException. Suppose I have a string variable that have characters, converting this variable into digit will occur NumberFormatException.

```
String s="abc";
int i=Integer.parseInt(s);//NumberFormatException
```

### *4) Scenario where ArrayIndexOutOfBoundsException Occurs*

If you are inserting any value in the wrong index, it would result

ArrayIndexOutOfBoundsException as shown below:

```
int a[]=new int[5];
a[10]=50; //ArrayIndexOutOfBoundsException
```

### *Java Exception Handling Keywords*

There are 5 keywords used in java exception handling.

1. try
2. catch
3. finally
4. throw
5. throws

### *Try Block*

Java try block is used to enclose the code that might throw an exception. It must be used within the method.

Java try block must be followed by either catch or finally block.

### *Syntax of Java Try-Catch*

```
try{
//code that may throw exception
}
catch(Exception_class_Name ref){}
```

### *Syntax of Try-Finally Block*

```
try{

//code that may throw exception

}

finally{}
```

**catch block**

Java catch block is used to handle the Exception. It must be used after the try block only.

You can use multiple catch block with a single try.

***Example***

```
public class Testtrycatch2{
public static void main(String args[]){
try{
        int data=50/0;
}catch(ArithmeticException e){System.out.println(e);}
System.out.println("rest of the code...");
}
}
```

Output:

Exception in thread main

java.lang.ArithmeticException:/ by zero rest of the code...

Now, as displayed in the above example, rest of the code is executed i.e. rest of the code...

statement is printed.

***Finally Block***

**Java finally block** is a block that is used *to execute important code* such as closing connection, stream etc.

Java finally block is always executed whether exception is handled or not.

Java finally block must be followed by try or catch block.

***Example***

```
public class TestFinallyBlock2{
public static void main(String args[]){
try{
        int data=25/0;
        System.out.println(data);
}
catch(ArithmeticException e){System.out.println(e);}
finally{System.out.println("finally block is always executed");}
System.out.println("rest of the code...");
}
}
```

***Output***

Exception in thread main java.lang.ArithmeticException:/ by zero finally block is always executed rest of the code...

### *throw keyword*

The Java throw keyword is used to explicitly throw an exception.

We can throw either checked or uncheked exception in java by throw keyword. The throw keyword is mainly used to throw custom exception. The syntax of java throw keyword is given below.

**throw** exception;

### *throw keyword Example*

In this example, we have created the validate method that takes integer value as a parameter. If the age is less than 18, we are throwing the ArithmeticException otherwise print a message welcome to vote.

```
public class TestThrow1{
    static void validate(int age){
        if(age<18)
        throw new ArithmeticException("not valid");
        else
        System.out.println("welcome to vote");
    }
    public static void main(String args[]){
        validate(13);
        System.out.println("rest of the code...");
}

}
```

***Output***

Exception in thread main java.lang.ArithmeticException:not valid

### *throws keyword*

The **Java throws keyword** is used to declare an exception. It gives an information to the programmer that there may occur an exception so it is better for the programmer to provide the exception handling code so that normal flow can be maintained.

### *Syntax of throws*

```
return_type method_name() throws exception_class_name{
...
}
```

### *throws example*

Let's see the example of java throws clause which describes that checked exceptions can be propagated by throws keyword.

```
import java.io.IOException;
class Testthrows1{
  void m()throws IOException{
   throw new IOException("device error");//checked exception

  }
  void n()throws IOException{
    m();
    }
  void p(){
   try{
    n();
   }catch(Exception e){System.out.println("exception handled");}
  }
  public static void main(String args[]){
   Testthrows1 obj=new Testthrows1();
   obj.p();
   System.out.println("normal flow...");
  }
}
```

### *Output*

```
exception handled
normal flow...
```

## 3.9. Exception Enrichment in Java

Exception enrichment is an alternative to **exception wrapping**.

In exception enrichment you do not wrap exceptions. Instead you add contextual information to the original exception and rethrow it. Rethrowing an exception does not reset the stack trace embedded in the exception.

Here is an example:

```
public void method2() throws EnrichableException{
  try{
    method1();
  }
  catch(EnrichableException e)
  {
     e.addInfo("An error occurred when trying to
    ...");
    throw e;
  }
}
public void method1() throws EnrichableException {
  if(...) throw new EnrichableException(
```

## 3.10. Assertion

Assertion is a statement in java. It can be used to test your assumptions about the program.

While executing assertion, it is believed to be true. If it fails, JVM will throw an error named AssertionError. It is mainly used for testing purpose.

### *Advantage of Assertion*

It provides an effective way to detect and correct programming errors.

### *Syntax of Using Assertion*

There are two ways to use assertion. First way is:

```
assert expression;
```

and second way is:

```
assert expression1 :
expression2;
```

Simple Example of Assertion in java:

```
import java.util.Scanner;
```

```
class AssertionExample{
 public static void main( String args[] ){
  Scanner scanner = new Scanner( System.in );
  System.out.print("Enter ur age ");
  int value = scanner.nextInt();
  assert value>=18:" Not valid";
  System.out.println("value is "+value);
 }
}
```

# CHAPTER IV

# Multithreading

## 4.1. Introduction to Multithreading

**Multithreading in java** is a process of executing multiple threads simultaneously.

Thread is basically a lightweight sub-process, a smallest unit of processing. Multiprocessing and multithreading, both are used to achieve multitasking.

But we use multithreading than multiprocessing because threads share a common memory area. They don't allocate separate memory area so saves memory, and context-switching between the threads takes less time than process.

Java Multithreading is mostly used in games, animation etc

Advantage of Java Multithreading

1) It **doesn't block the user** because threads are independent and you can perform multiple operations at same time.
2) You **can perform many operations together so it saves time**.
3) Threads are **independent** so it doesn't affect other threads if exception occur in a single thread.

### *Multitasking*

Multitasking is a process of executing multiple tasks simultaneously. We use multitasking to utilize the CPU. Multitasking can be achieved by two ways:

- Process-based Multitasking(Multiprocessing)
- Thread-based Multitasking(Multithreading)

1) Process-based Multitasking (Multiprocessing)
   - Each process have its own address in memory i.e. each process allocates separate memory area.
   - Process is heavyweight.
   - Cost of communication between the processes is high.
   - Switching from one process to another require some time for saving and loading registers, memory maps, updating lists etc.
2) Thread-based Multitasking (Multithreading)
   - Threads share the same address space.

- Thread is lightweight.
- Cost of communication between the thread is low.

## 4.2. What is Thread in Java

A thread is a lightweight sub process, a smallest unit of processing. It is a separate path of execution.

Threads are independent, if there occurs exception in one thread, it doesn't affect other threads. It shares a common memory area.

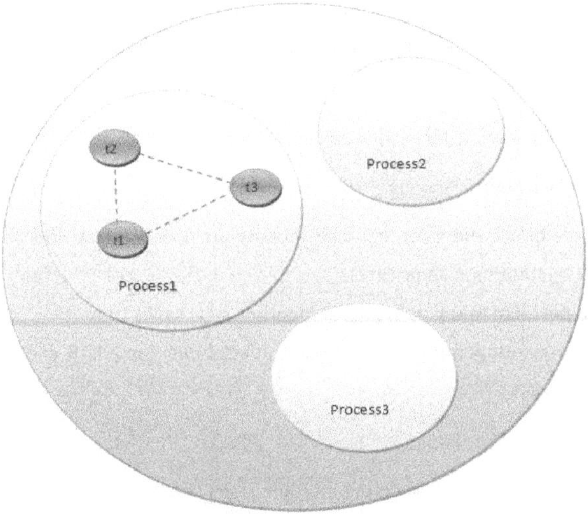


OS

## 4.3. Life Cycle of a Thread (Thread States)

A thread can be in one of the five states. According to sun, there is only 4 states in **thread life cycle in java** new, runnable, non-runnable and terminated. There is no running state.

But for better understanding the threads, we are explaining it in the 5 states.

The life cycle of the thread in java is controlled by JVM. The java thread states are as follows:

1. New
2. Runnable
3. Running

4. Non-Runnable (Blocked)z
5. Terminated

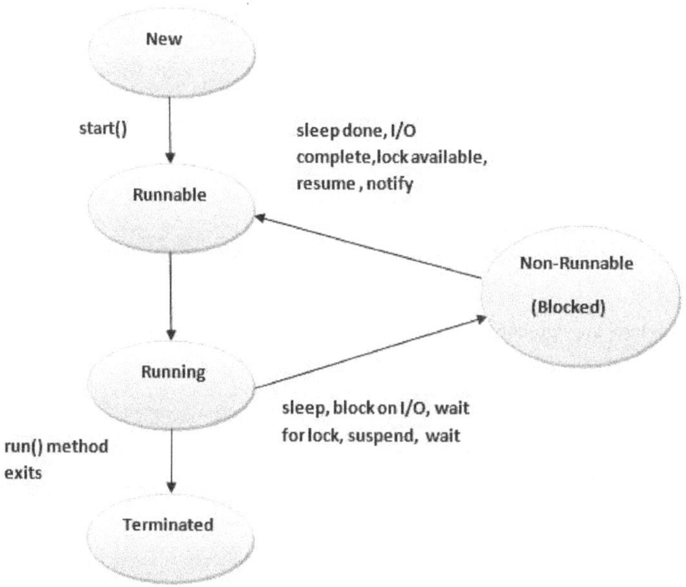


### *1) New*

The thread is in new state if you create an instance of Thread class but before the invocation of start() method.

### *2) Runnable*

The thread is in runnable state after invocation of start() method, but the thread scheduler has not selected it to be the running thread.

### *3) Running*

The thread is in running state if the thread scheduler has selected it.

4) Non-Runnable (Blocked)

This is the state when the thread is still alive, but is currently not eligible to run.

### *5) Terminated*

A thread is in terminated or dead state when its run() method exits.

### *How to Create Thread*

There are two ways to create a thread:

1. By extending Thread class
2. By implementing Runnable interface.

### *How to Create Thread*

There are two ways to create a thread:

1. By extending Thread class
2. By implementing Runnable interface.

### *Thread Class*

Thread class provide constructors and methods to create and perform operations on a thread. Thread class extends Object class and implements Runnable interface.

Commonly used Constructors of Thread class:

- Thread()
- Thread(String name)
- Thread(Runnable r)
- Thread(Runnable r, String name)

### *Commonly Used Methods of Thread Class*

1. **public void run():** is used to perform action for a thread.
2. **public void start():** starts the execution of the thread.JVM calls the run() method on the thread.
3. **public void sleep(long milliseconds):** Causes the currently executing thread to sleep (temporarily cease execution) for the specified number of milliseconds.
4. **public void join():** waits for a thread to die.
5. **public void join(long milliseconds):** waits for a thread to die for the specified milliseconds.
6. **public int getPriority():** returns the priority of the thread.
7. **public int setPriority(int priority):** changes the priority of the thread.
8. **public String getName():** returns the name of the thread.
9. **public void setName(String name):** changes the name of the thread.
10. **public Thread currentThread():** returns the reference of currently executing thread.
11. **public int getId():** returns the id of the thread.

12. **public Thread.State getState():** returns the state of the thread.
13. **public boolean isAlive():** tests if the thread is alive.
14. **public void yield():** causes the currently executing thread object to temporarily pause and allow other threads to execute.
15. **public void suspend():** is used to suspend the thread(depricated).
16. **public void resume():** is used to resume the suspended thread(depricated).
17. **public void stop():** is used to stop the thread(depricated).
18. **public boolean isDaemon():** tests if the thread is a daemon thread.
19. **public void setDaemon(boolean b):** marks the thread as daemon or user thread.
20. **public void interrupt():** interrupts the thread.
21. **public boolean isInterrupted():** tests if the thread has been interrupted.
22. **public static boolean interrupted():** tests if the current thread has been interrupted.

## 4.4. Runnable Interface

The Runnable interface should be implemented by any class whose instances are intended to be executed by a thread. Runnable interface have only one method named run().

1. **public void run():** is used to perform action for a thread.

***Starting a Thread***

**start() method** of Thread class is used to start a newly created thread. It performs following tasks:

- A new thread starts(with new callstack).
- The thread moves from New state to the Runnable state.
- When the thread gets a chance to execute, its target run() method will run.

1. By extending Thread class:

```
class Multi extends Thread{
public void run(){
System.out.println("thread is running...");
}
public static void main(String args[]){
Multi t1=new Multi();
t1.start();
}
}
```

Output: thread is running...

### *Who Makes Your Class Object as Thread Object?*

**Thread class constructor** allocates a new thread object. When you create object of Multi class, your class constructor is invoked (provided by Compiler) from where Thread class constructor is invoked(by super() as first statement).So your Multi class object is thread object now.

2. By implementing the Runnable interface:

```
class Multi3 implements Runnable{
public void run(){
System.out.println("thread is running...");
}
public static void main(String args[]){
Multi3 m1=new Multi3();
Thread t1 =new Thread(m1);
t1.start();
 }
}
```

Output: thread is running...

If you are not extending the Thread class, your class object would not be treated as a thread object. So you need to explicitly create Thread class object. We are passing the object of your class that implements Runnable so that your class run() method may execute.

Priority of a Thread (Thread Priority):

Each thread has a priority. Priorities are represented by a number between 1 and 10. In most cases, thread scheduler schedules the threads according to their priority (known as preemptive scheduling).

But it is not guaranteed because it depends on JVM specification that which scheduling it chooses.

## 4.5. Thread Class

1. public static int MIN_PRIORITY
2. public static int NORM_PRIORITY
3. public static int MAX_PRIORITY

Default priority of a thread is 5 (NORM_PRIORITY). The value of MIN_PRIORITY is 1 and the value of MAX_PRIORITY is 10.

### *Example of Priority of a Thread*

```
class TestMultiPriority1 extends Thread{
public void run(){
System.out.println("running thread name is:"+Thread.currentThread().getName());
System.out.println("running thread priority is:"+Thread.currentThread().getPriority());
}
public static void main(String args[]){
TestMultiPriority1 m1=new TestMultiPriority1();
TestMultiPriority1 m2=new TestMultiPriority1();
m1.setPriority(Thread.MIN_PRIORITY);
m2.setPriority(Thread.MAX_PRIORITY);
m1.start();
m2.start();
}
}
```

Output: running thread name is: Thread-0

running thread priority is:10

running thread name is:Thread-1

running thread priority is:1

### *Joining Threads*

Sometimes one thread needs to know when another thread is ending. In java, **isAlive()** and **join()** are two different methods to check whether a thread has finished its execution.

The **isAlive()** methods return **true** if the thread upon which it is called is still running otherwise it return **false**.

*final* boolean **isAlive()**

But, **join()** method is used more commonly than **isAlive()**. This method waits until the thread on which it is called terminates.

*final* void **join()** throws **InterruptedException**

Using **join()** method, we tell our thread to wait until the specifid thread completes its execution. There are overloaded versions of **join()** method, which allows us to specify time for which you want to wait for the specified thread to terminate.

*final* void **join**(long *milliseconds*) throws **InterruptedException**

***Example of isAlive method***

```
public class MyThread extends Thread
{
public void run()
  {
     System.out.println("r1 ");
     try{
      Thread.sleep(500);
   }catch(InterruptedException ie){}
     System.out.println("r2 ");
  }
public static void main(String[] args)
{
MyThread t1=new MyThread();
MyThread t2=new MyThread();
t1.start();
t2.start();
System.out.println(t1.isAlive());
System.out.println(t2.isAlive());
}
}
```

***Output***

```
r1
true
true
r1
r2
r2
```

***Example of thread without join() method***

```
public class MyThread extends Thread
{
public void run()
  {
```

```
        System.out.println("r1 ");
        try{
         Thread.sleep(500);
    }catch(InterruptedException ie){}
        System.out.println("r2 ");
  }
public static void main(String[] args)
{
MyThread t1=new MyThread();
MyThread t2=new MyThread();
t1.start();
t2.start();
}
}
```

***Output***

```
r1
r1
r2
r2
```

In this above program two thread t1 and t2 are created. t1 starts first and after printing "r1" on console thread t1 goes to sleep for 500 mls.At the same time Thread t2 will start its process and print "r1" on console and then goes into sleep for 500 mls. Thread t1 will wake up from sleep and print "r2" on console similarly thread t2 will wake up from sleep and print "r2" on console. So you will get output like r1 r1 r2 r2

***Example of thread with join() method***

```
public class MyThread extends Thread
{
public void run()
  {
        System.out.println("r1 ");
        try{
         Thread.sleep(500);
    }catch(InterruptedException ie){}
```

```
    System.out.println("r2 ");
 }
public static void main(String[] args)
{
MyThread t1=new MyThread();
MyThread t2=new MyThread();
t1.start();
try{
 t1.join(); //Waiting for t1 to finish
}catch(InterruptedException ie){}
t2.start();
}
}
```

***Output***

```
r1
r2
r1
r2
```

In this above program join() method on thread t1 ensure that t1 finishes it process before thread t2 starts.

## *Specifying time with join()*

If in the above program, we specify time while using **join()** with **m1**, then **m1** will execute for that time, and then**m2** and **m3** will join it.

**m1.join(1500);**

Doing so, initially m1 will execute for 1.5 seconds, after which m2 and m3 will join it.

In the last chapter we have seen the ways of naming thread in java. In this chapter we will be learning the different priorities that a thread can have.

Java Thread Priority :

1. Logically we can say that threads run simultaneously but practically its not true, only one Thread can run at a time in such a ways that user feels that concurrent environment.

2. Fixed priority scheduling algorithm is used to select one thread for execution based on priority.

***Example #1: Default Thread Priority***

**getPriority()** method is used to get the priority of the thread.

```
package com.c4learn.thread;
public class ThreadPriority extends Thread {
 public void run() {
  System.out.println(Thread.currentThread().getPriority());
 }
 public static void main(String[] args)
                throws InterruptedException {
  ThreadPriority t1 = new ThreadPriority();
  ThreadPriority t2 = new ThreadPriority();
  t1.start();
  t2.start();
 }
}
```

Output :

5

5

default priority of the thread is 5.

Each thread has normal priority at the time of creation. We can change or modify the thread priority in the following example 2.

Example #2 : Setting Priority

```
package com.c4learn.thread;
public class ThreadPriority extends Thread {
 public void run() {
  String tName = Thread.currentThread().getName();
  Integer tPrio = Thread.currentThread().getPriority();
  System.out.println(tName + " has priority " + tPrio);
 }
 public static void main(String[] args) throws InterruptedException {
  ThreadPriority t0 = new ThreadPriority();
  ThreadPriority t1 = new ThreadPriority();
```

```
    ThreadPriority t2 = new ThreadPriority();
    t1.setPriority(Thread.MAX_PRIORITY);
    t0.setPriority(Thread.MIN_PRIORITY);
    t2.setPriority(Thread.NORM_PRIORITY);
    t0.start();
    t1.start();
    t2.start();
  }
}
```

***Output***

```
Thread-0 has priority 1
Thread-2 has priority 5
Thread-1 has priority 10
```

Explanation of Thread Priority:

1. We can modify the thread priority using the **setPriority()** method.
2. Thread can have integer priority between 1 to 10
3. Java Thread class defines following constants.
4. At a time many thread can be ready for execution but the thread with highest priority is selected for execution
5. Thread have default priority equal to 5.

Thread: Priority and Constant

| Thread Priority | Constant |
|---|---|
| MIN_PRIORITY | 1 |
| MAX_PRIORITY | 10 |
| NORM_PRIORITY | 5 |

## 4.6. Java Thread Synchronization

1. In multi-threading environment, When two or more threads need access to a any shared resource then their should be some mechanism to ensure that the resource will be used by only one thread at a time.
2. Thread Synchronization is a process by which this synchronization is achieved.

3. Thread Synchronization is used to prevent thread interference and consistency problem.
4. Thread Synchronization is achieved through keyword **synchronized**.

### *4.6.1. Types of Synchronization*

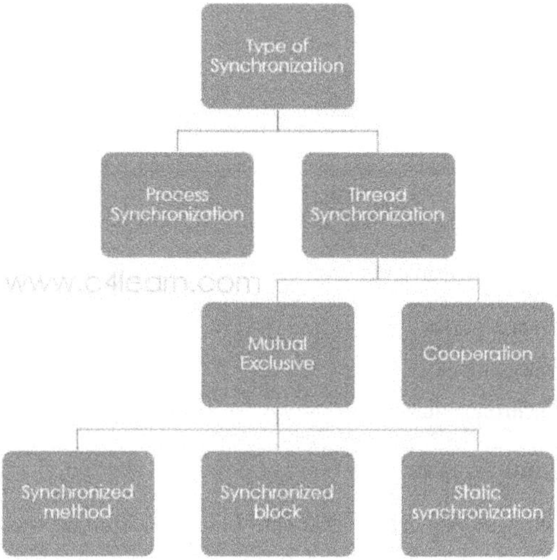


### *Synchronization in Java*

Synchronization in java is the capability *to control the access of multiple threads to any shared resource.* Java Synchronization is better option where we want to allow only one thread to access the shared resource.

### *Why use Synchronization*

The synchronization is mainly used to

1. To prevent thread interference.
2. To prevent consistency problem.

### *Types of Synchronization*

There are two types of synchronization

1. Process Synchronization
2. Thread Synchronization

Here, we will discuss only thread synchronization.

### *Thread Synchronization*

There are two types of thread synchronization mutual exclusive and inter-thread communication.

1. Mutual Exclusive
    1. Synchronized method.
    2. Synchronized block.
    3. Static synchronization.
2. Cooperation (Inter-thread communication in java)

### *Mutual Exclusive*

Mutual Exclusive helps keep threads from interfering with one another while sharing data.

This can be done by three ways in java:

1. by synchronized method
2. by synchronized block
3. by static synchronization

## 4.7. Concept of Lock in Java

Synchronization is built around an internal entity known as the lock or monitor. Every object has an lock associated with it. By convention, a thread that needs consistent access to an object's fields has to acquire the object's lock before accessing them, and then release the lock when it's done with them.

From Java 5 the package java.util.concurrent.locks contains several lock implementations.

Understanding the problem without Synchronization

In this example, there is no synchronization, so output is inconsistent. Let's see the example:

```
Class Table{
void printTable(int n){//method not synchronized
  for(int i=1;i<=5;i++){
   System.out.println(n*i);
   try{
    Thread.sleep(400);
   }catch(Exception e){System.out.println(e);}
  }
```

```
 }
}
class MyThread1 extends Thread{
Table t;
MyThread1(Table t){
this.t=t;
}
public void run(){
t.printTable(5);
}
}
class MyThread2 extends Thread{
Table t;
MyThread2(Table t){
this.t=t;
}
public void run(){
t.printTable(100);
}
}
class TestSynchronization1{
public static void main(String args[]){
Table obj = new Table();//only one object
MyThread1 t1=new MyThread1(obj);
MyThread2 t2=new MyThread2(obj);
t1.start();
t2.start();
}
}
```

Output: 5

100

10

200

15

```
300
20
400
25
500
```

### *Java Synchronized Method*

If you declare any method as synchronized, it is known as synchronized method.

Synchronized method is used to lock an object for any shared resource.

When a thread invokes a synchronized method, it automatically acquires the lock for that object and releases it when the thread completes its task.

```
//example of java synchronized method
class Table{
 synchronized void printTable(int n){//synchronized method
   for(int i=1;i<=5;i++){
     System.out.println(n*i);
     try{
      Thread.sleep(400);
     }catch(Exception e){System.out.println(e);}
   }
 }
}
class MyThread1 extends Thread{
Table t;
MyThread1(Table t){
this.t=t;
}
public void run(){
t.printTable(5);
}
}
class MyThread2 extends Thread{
Table t;
MyThread2(Table t){
```

```
this.t=t;
}
public void run(){
t.printTable(100);
}
}
public class TestSynchronization2{
public static void main(String args[]){
Table obj = new Table();//only one object
MyThread1 t1=new MyThread1(obj);
MyThread2 t2=new MyThread2(obj);
t1.start();
t2.start();
}
}
```

Output: 5

```
10
15
20
25
100
200
300
400
500
```

Example of synchronized method by using annonymous class

In this program, we have created the two threads by annonymous class, so less coding is required.

```
//Program of synchronized method by using annonymous class
class Table{
 synchronized void printTable(int n){//synchronized method
  for(int i=1;i<=5;i++){
   System.out.println(n*i);
   try{
```

```
      Thread.sleep(400);
     }catch(Exception e){System.out.println(e);}
   }
  }
 }
 public class TestSynchronization3{
 public static void main(String args[]){
 final Table obj = new Table();//only one object
 Thread t1=new Thread(){
 public void run(){
 obj.printTable(5);
 }
 };
 Thread t2=new Thread(){
 public void run(){
 obj.printTable(100);
 }
 };
 t1.start();
 t2.start();
 }
 }
```

Output: 5

```
10
15
20
25
100
200
300
400
500
```

## 4.8. Synchronized Block in Java

Synchronized block can be used to perform synchronization on any specific resource of the method.

Suppose you have 50 lines of code in your method, but you want to synchronize only 5 lines, you can use synchronized block.

If you put all the codes of the method in the synchronized block, it will work same as the synchronized method.

### *Points to Remember for Synchronized Block*

- Synchronized block is used to lock an object for any shared resource.
- Scope of synchronized block is smaller than the method.

### *Syntax to Use Synchronized Block*

```
synchronized (object reference expression) {
  //code block
}
```

Example of synchronized block

Let's see the simple example of synchronized block.

***Program of synchronized block***

```
class Table{
 void printTable(int n){
   synchronized(this){//synchronized block
     for(int i=1;i<=5;i++){
      System.out.println(n*i);
      try{
       Thread.sleep(400);
      }catch(Exception e)
      {
      System.out.println(e);
      }
     }
   }
 }//end of the method
}
```

```
class MyThread1 extends Thread{
Table t;
MyThread1(Table t){
this.t=t;
}
public void run(){
t.printTable(5);
}
}
class MyThread2 extends Thread{
Table t;
MyThread2(Table t){
this.t=t;
}
public void run(){
t.printTable(100);
}
}
public class TestSynchronizedBlock1{
public static void main(String args[]){
Table obj = new Table();//only one object
MyThread1 t1=new MyThread1(obj);
MyThread2 t2=new MyThread2(obj);
t1.start();
t2.start();
}
}
```

Output:5

10

15

20

25

100

200

```
300
400
500
```

Same Example of synchronized block by using annonymous class:

***//Program of synchronized block by using annonymous class***

```
class Table{
 void printTable(int n){
  synchronized(this){//synchronized block
   for(int i=1;i<=5;i++){
    System.out.println(n*i);
    try{
     Thread.sleep(400);
    }catch(Exception e){System.out.println(e);}
   }
  }
}//end of the method
}
public class TestSynchronizedBlock2{
public static void main(String args[]){
final Table obj = new Table();//only one object
Thread t1=new Thread(){
public void run(){
obj.printTable(5);
}
};
Thread t2=new Thread(){
public void run(){
obj.printTable(100);
}
};
t1.start();
t2.start();
}
}
```

Output:5

10

15

20

25

100

200

300

400

500

### *Static Synchronization*

If you make any static method as synchronized, the lock will be on the class not on object.

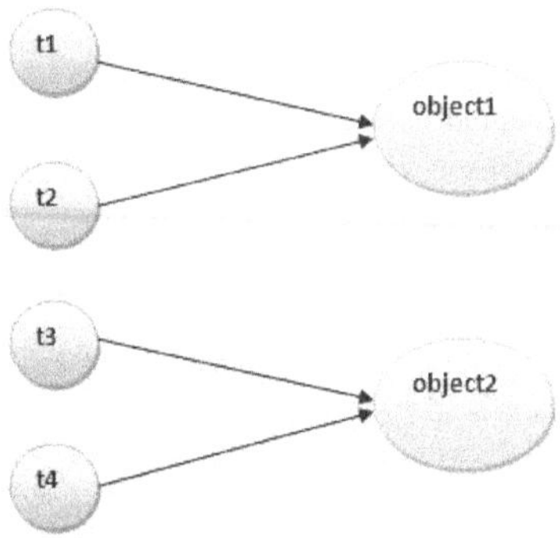


### *Problem without Static Synchronization*

Suppose there are two objects of a shared class(e.g. Table) named object1 and object2.In case of synchronized method and synchronized block there cannot be interference between t1 and t2 or t3 and t4 because t1 and t2 both refers to a common object that have a single lock. But there can be interference between t1 and t3 or t2 and t4 because t1 acquires another lock and t3 acquires another lock. I want no interference between t1 and t3 or t2 and t4.Static synchronization solves this problem.

### *Example of Static Synchronization*

In this example we are applying synchronized keyword on the static method to perform static synchronization.

```
class Table{
 synchronized static void printTable(int n){
   for(int i=1;i<=10;i++){
     System.out.println(n*i);
     try{
       Thread.sleep(400);
     }catch(Exception e){}
   }
 }
}
class MyThread1 extends Thread{
public void run(){
Table.printTable(1);
}
}
class MyThread2 extends Thread{
public void run(){
Table.printTable(10);
}
}
class MyThread3 extends Thread{
public void run(){
Table.printTable(100);
}
}
class MyThread4 extends Thread{
public void run(){
Table.printTable(1000);
}
}
public class TestSynchronization4{
public static void main(String t[]){
MyThread1 t1=new MyThread1();
MyThread2 t2=new MyThread2();
```

```
MyThread3 t3=new MyThread3();
MyThread4 t4=new MyThread4();
t1.start();
t2.start();
t3.start();
t4.start();
}
}
```

Output: 1

```
2
3
4
5
6
7
8
9
10
10
20
30
40
50
60
70
80
90
100
100
200
300
400
500
600
```

```
700
800
900
1000
1000
2000
3000
4000
5000
6000
7000
8000
9000
10000
```

Same example of static synchronization by annonymous class

In this example, we are using annonymous class to create the threads.

```
class Table{
 synchronized static void printTable(int n){
   for(int i=1;i<=10;i++){
     System.out.println(n*i);
     try{
       Thread.sleep(400);
     }catch(Exception e){}
   }
 }
}
 public class TestSynchronization5 {
public static void main(String[] args) {
    Thread t1=new Thread(){
        public void run(){
            Table.printTable(1);
        }
    };
    Thread t2=new Thread(){
```

```
            public void run(){
                Table.printTable(10);
            }
        };
        Thread t3=new Thread(){
            public void run(){
                Table.printTable(100);
            }
        };
        Thread t4=new Thread(){
            public void run(){
                Table.printTable(1000);
            }
        };
        t1.start();
        t2.start();
        t3.start();
        t4.start();
    }
}
```

```
Output: 1
    2
    3
    4
    5
    6
    7
    8
    9
    10
    10
    20
    30
    40
```

```
50
60
70
80
90
100
100
200
300
400
500
600
700
800
900
1000
1000
2000
3000
4000
5000
6000
7000
8000
9000
10000
```

## 4.9. Synchronized Block on a Class Lock

The block synchronizes on the lock of the object denoted by the reference .class name .class. A static synchronized method printTable(int n) in class Table is equivalent to the following declaration:

```
static void printTable(int n) {
   synchronized (Table.class) { // Synchronized block on class A// ...
   }
}
```

### *Introduction to Suspend Resume Thread*

When the **sleep()** method time is over, the thread becomes implicitly active. **sleep()** method is preferable when the inactive time is known earlier. Sometimes, the inactive time or blocked time may not be known to the programmer earlier; to come to the task here comes **suspend()**method. The suspended thread will be in blocked state until **resume()** method is called on it. These methods are deprecated, as when not used With precautions, the thread locks, if held, are kept in inconsistent state or may lead to deadlocks.

**Note:** You must have noticed, in the earlier **sleep()** method, that the thread in blocked state retains all its state. That is, attribute values remains unchanged by the time it comes into runnable state.

**Suspend Resume Thread: Program explaining the usage of suspend() and resume() methods**

```
public class SRDemo extends Thread
{
 public static void main( String args[ ] )
 {
   SRDemo srd1 = new SRDemo();
   SRDemo srd2 = new SRDemo();
   srd1.setName("First");
   srd2.setName("Second");
   srd1.start();
   srd2.start();
   try
   {
     Thread.sleep( 1000 );
     srd1.suspend();
     System.out.println("Suspending thread First");
     Thread.sleep( 1000 );
     srd1.resume();
     System.out.println("Resuming thread First");
     Thread.sleep(1000);
     srd2.suspend();
     System.out.println("Suspending thread Second");
     Thread.sleep(1000);
```

```
    srd2.resume();
    System.out.println("Resuming thread Second");
  }
  catch(InterruptedException e)
  {
    e.printStackTrace();
  }
 }
 public void run()
 {
  try
  {
  for(int i=0; i<7; i++)
  {
    Thread.sleep(500);
    System.out.println( this.getName() + ": " + i );
  }
  }
  catch(InterruptedException e)
  {
   e.printStackTrace();
  }
 }
}
```

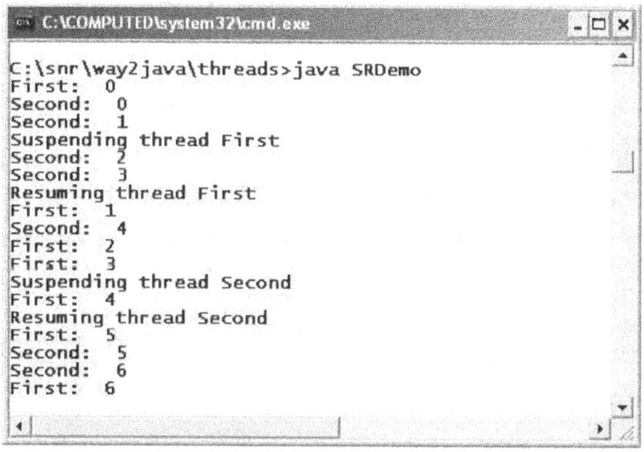

### *Output Screen on Suspend Resume Thread Java*

Observe the screenshot, when no thread is suspended both threads are under execution. When **First** thread goes into suspended state, the **Second** thread goes into action. Similarly, when the **Second** goes to suspended state, the **First** is executed.

## 4.10. Inter-thread Communication in Java

**Inter-thread communication** or **Co-operation** is all about allowing synchronized threads to communicate with each other.

Cooperation (Inter-thread communication) is a mechanism in which a thread is paused running in its critical section and another thread is allowed to enter (or lock) in the same critical section to be executed. It is implemented by following methods of **Object class**:

- wait()
- notify()
- notifyAll()

### *1. wait() method*

Causes current thread to release the lock and wait until either another thread invokes the notify() method or the notifyAll() method for this object, or a specified amount of time has elapsed.

The current thread must own this object's monitor, so it must be called from the synchronized method only otherwise it will throw exception.

| Method | Description |
|---|---|
| public final void wait()throws InterruptedException | waits until object is notified. |
| public final void wait(long timeout)throws InterruptedException | waits for the specified amount of time. |

### *2. notify() method*

Wakes up a single thread that is waiting on this object's monitor. If any threads are waiting on this object, one of them is chosen to be awakened. The choice is arbitrary and occurs at the discretion of the implementation.

### *Syntax*

public final void notify()

**3) notifyAll() method**

Wakes up all threads that are waiting on this object's monitor.

***Syntax***

public final void notifyAll()

***Understanding the Process of Inter-thread Communication***

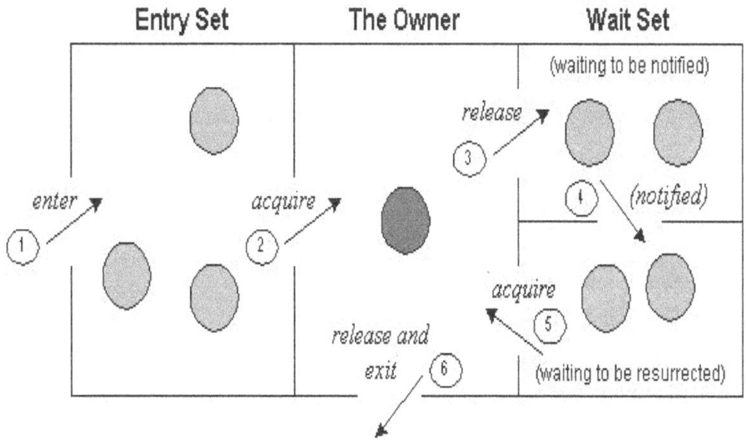


The point to point explanation of the above diagram is as follows:

1. Threads enter to acquire lock.
2. Lock is acquired by on thread.
3. Now thread goes to waiting state if you call wait() method on the object. Otherwise it releases the lock and exits.
4. If you call notify() or notifyAll() method, thread moves to the notified state (runnable state).
5. Now thread is available to acquire lock.
6. After completion of the task, thread releases the lock and exits the monitor state of the object.

Why wait(), notify() and notifyAll() methods are defined in Object class not Thread class?

It is because they are related to lock and object has a lock.

Difference between wait and sleep?

Let's see the important differences between wait and sleep methods.

| wait() | sleep() |
|---|---|
| wait() method releases the lock | sleep() method doesn't release the lock. |
| is the method of Object class | is the method of Thread class |
| is the non-static method | is the static method |
| is the non-static method | is the static method |
| should be notified by notify() or notifyAll() methods | after the specified amount of time, sleep is completed. |

### *Example of Inter Thread Communication in Java*

Let's see the simple example of inter thread communication.

```
class Customer{
int amount=10000;
synchronized void withdraw(int amount){
System.out.println("going to withdraw...");
if(this.amount<amount){
System.out.println("Less balance; waiting for deposit...");
try{wait();}catch(Exception e){}
}
this.amount-=amount;
System.out.println("withdraw completed...");
}
synchronized void deposit(int amount){
System.out.println("going to deposit...");
this.amount+=amount;
System.out.println("deposit completed... ");
notify();
}
}
class Test{
public static void main(String args[]){
final Customer c=new Customer();
new Thread(){
public void run(){c.withdraw(15000);}
}.start();
```

```
new Thread(){
public void run(){c.deposit(10000);}
}
start();
}}
```

Output: going to withdraw...

Less balance; waiting for deposit...

going to deposit...

deposit completed...

withdraw completed

## 4.11. IO Stream

Java performs I/O through **Streams**. A Stream is linked to a physical layer by java I/O system to make input and output operation in java. In general, a stream means continuous flow of data. Streams are clean way to deal with input/output without having every part of your code understand the physical.

Java encapsulates Stream under **java.io** package. Java defines two types of streams. They are,

1. **Byte Stream :** It provides a convenient means for handling input and output of byte.
2. **Character Stream :** It provides a convenient means for handling input and output of characters. Character stream uses Unicode and therefore can be internationalized.

### *Byte Stream Classes*

Byte stream is defined by using two abstract class at the top of hierarchy, they are InputStream and OutputStream.

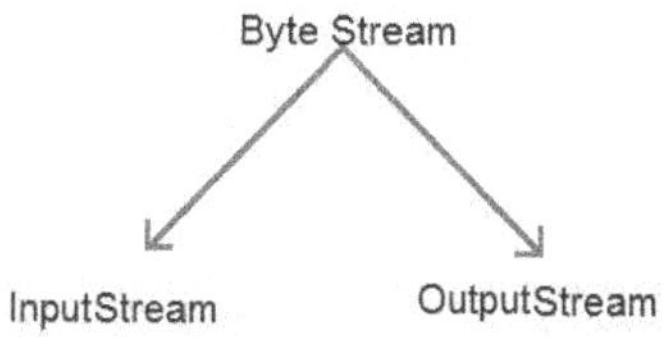


These two abstract classes have several concrete classes that handle various devices such as disk files, network connection etc.

**Some important Byte stream classes.**

| Stream class | Description |
|---|---|
| **BufferedInputStream** | Used for Buffered Input Stream. |
| **BufferedOutputStream** | Used for Buffered Output Stream. |
| **DataInputStream** | Contains method for reading java standard datatype |
| **DataOutputStream** | An output stream that contain method for writing java standard data type |
| **FileInputStream** | Input stream that reads from a file |
| **FileOutputStream** | Output stream that write to a file. |
| **InputStream** | Abstract class that describe stream input. |
| **OutputStream** | Abstract class that describe stream output. |
| **PrintStream** | Output Stream that contain print() and println() method |

These classes define several key methods. Two most important are:

read() : reads byte of data.

1. write(): Writes byte of data.

### *Character Stream Classes*

Character stream is also defined by using two abstract class at the top of hierarchy, they are Reader and Writer.

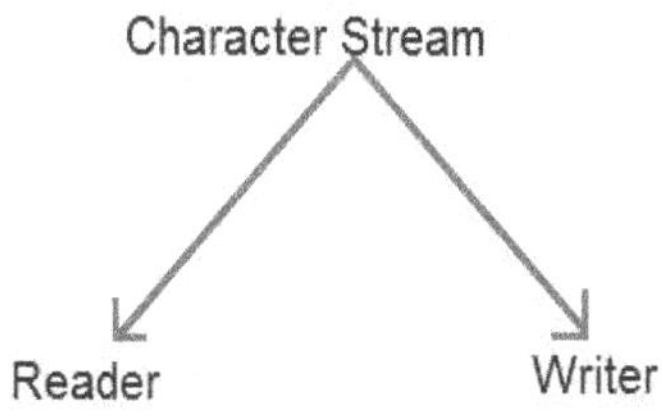


These two abstract classes have several concrete classes that handle unicode character.

**Some important Charcter stream classes.**

| Stream class | Description |
|---|---|
| **BufferedReader** | Handles buffered input stream. |
| **BufferedWriter** | Handles buffered output stream. |
| **FileReader** | Input stream that reads from file. |
| **FileWriter** | Output stream that writes to file. |
| **InputStreamReader** | Input stream that translate byte to character |
| **OutputStreamReader** | Output stream that translate character to byte. |
| **PrintWriter** | Output Stream that contain print() and println() method. |
| **Reader** | Abstract class that define character stream input |
| **Writer** | Abstract class that define character stream output |

## *Reading Console Input*

We use the object of BufferedReader class to take inputs from the keyboard.

Object of BufferedReader class

```
BufferedReader br = new BufferedReader(new
                    InputStreamReader (System.in) );
```

*InputStreamReader* is subclass of Reader class. It converts bytes to character.

Console inputs are read from this.

### *Reading Characters*

read() method is used with BufferedReader object to read characters. As this function returns integer type value has we need to use typecasting to convert it into **char** type.

*int* **read()** throws **IOException**

Below is a simple example explaining character input.

```
class CharRead
{
 public static void main( String args[])
 {
  BufferedReader br = new Bufferedreader(new InputstreamReader(System.in));
 char c = (char)br.read(); //Reading character }
}
```

### *Reading Strings*

To read string we have to use readLine() function with BufferedReader class's object. *String* **readLine()** throws **IOException**

**Program to take String input from Keyboard in Java**

```
import java.io.*;
class MyInput
{
 public static void main(String[] args)
 {
  String text;
  InputStreamReader isr = new InputStreamReader(System.in);
  BufferedReader br = new BufferedReader(isr);
```

```
 text = br.readLine();             //Reading String
 System.out.println(text);
 }
}
```

***Program to read from a file using BufferedReader class***

```
import java. Io *;
class ReadTest
{
 public static void main(String[] args)
 {
  try
  {
   File fl = new File("d:/myfile.txt");
   BufferedReader    br    =    new    BufferedReader(new
   FileReader(fl)) ; String str;
   while ((str=br.readLine())!=null)
   {
    System.out.println(str);
   }
   br.close();
   fl.close();
  }
  catch (IOException e)
  { e.printStackTrace(); }
 }
}
```

***Program to write to a File using FileWriter class***

```
import java. Io *;
class WriteTest
{
 public static void main(String[] args)
{
  try
```

```
{
 File fl = new File("d:/myfile.txt");
 String str="Write this string to my file";
 FileWriter fw = new FileWriter(fl) ;
 fw.write(str);
 fw.close();
 fl.close();
}
catch (IOException e)
{ e.printStackTrace(); }
}
}
```

# CHAPTER V

# Applets

## 5.1. Daemon Threads

- Any Java thread can be a *daemon* thread.
- Daemon threads are service providers for other threads running in the same process as the daemon thread.
- The run() method for a daemon thread is typically an infinite loop that waits for a service request. When the only remaining threads in a process are daemon threads, the interpreter exits. This makes sense because when only daemon threads remain, there is no other thread for which a daemon thread can provide a service.
- To specify that a thread is a daemon thread, call the setDaemon method with the argument true. To determine if a thread is a daemon thread, use the accessor method is Daemon.

## 5.2. Concepts of Applets

- *Applets* are small applications that are accessed on an Internet server, transported over the Internet, automatically installed, and run as part of a Web document.
- After an applet arrives on the client, it has limited access to resources, so that it can produce an arbitrary multimedia user interface and run complex computations without introducing the risk of viruses or breaching data integrity.
- applets – Java program that runs within a Java-enabled browser, invoked through a ―applet‖ reference on a web page, dynamically downloaded to the client computer

```
import java.awt.*;
import java.applet.*;
public class SimpleApplet extends Applet {
public void paint(Graphics g) {
g.drawString("A Simple Applet", 20, 20);
}
}
```

***There are Two Ways to Run An Applet***

1. Executing the applet within a Java-compatible Web browser, such as NetscapeNavigator.

2. Using an applet viewer, such as the standard JDK tool, **appletviewer**.

- An applet viewer executes your applet in a window. This is generally the fastest and easiest way to test an applet.
- To execute an applet in a Web browser, you need to write a short HTML text file that contains the appropriate APPLET tag.

```
<applet code="SimpleApplet" width=200
height=60> </applet>
```

***Differences between Applets and Applications***

- Java can be used to create two types of programs: applications and applets.
- An *application* is a program that runs on your computer, under the operating system of that Computer(i.e an application created by Java is more or less like one created using C or C++).
- When used to create applications, Java is not much different from any other computer language.
- An *applet* is an application designed to be transmitted over the Internet and executed by a Java-compatible Web browser.
- An applet is actually a tiny Java program, dynamically downloaded across the network, just like an image, sound file, or video clip.
- The important difference is that an applet is an *intelligent program*, not just an animation or media file(i.e an applet is a program that can react to user input and dynamically change—not just run the same animation or sound over and over
- Applications require main method to execute.
- Applets do not require main method.
- Java's console input is quite limited
- Applets are graphical and window-based.

## 5.3. Life Cycle of an Applet

- Applets life cycle includes the following methods
  1. **init( )**
  2. **start( )**
  3. **paint( )**
  4. **stop( )**
  5. **destroy( )**
- When an applet begins, the AWT calls the following methods, in this sequence:

**init( ) start( ) paint( )**

- When an applet is terminated, the following sequence of method calls takes place:

**stop() destroy( )**

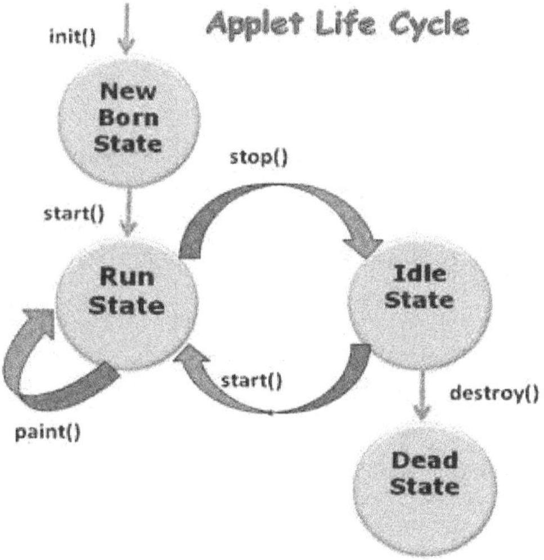


- **init( ):** The **init( )** method is the first method to be called. This is where you should initialize variables. This method is called only once during the run time of your applet.
- **start( ):** The **start( )** method is called after **init( )**. It is also called to restart an applet after it has been stopped. Whereas **init( )** is called once—the first time an applet is loaded—**start( )** is called each time an applet's HTML document is displayed onscreen. So, if a user leaves a web page and comes back, the applet resumes execution at **start( )**.
- **paint( ):** The **paint( )** method is called each time applet's output must be redrawn. **paint( )** is also called when the applet begins execution. Whatever the cause, whenever the applet must redraw its output, **paint( )** is called. The **paint( )** method has one parameter of type **Graphics**. This parameter will contain the graphics context, which describes the graphics environment in which the applet is running. This context is used whenever output to the applet is required.
- **stop( ):** The **stop( )** method is called when a web browser leaves the HTML document containing the applet—when it goes to another page, for example. When **stop( )** is called, the applet is probably running. Applet uses **stop( )** to suspend threads that

don't need to run when the applet is not visible. To restart **start( )** is called if the user returns to the page.

- **destroy( ):** The **destroy( )** method is called when the environment determines that your applet needs to be removed completely from memory. The **stop( )** method is always called before **destroy( )**.

**public void paint(Graphics g)**

- Needed if you do any drawing or painting other than just using standard GUI Components
- Any painting you want to do should be done here, or in a method you call from here.
- Painting that you do in other methods may *or may not* happen*Never call* paint(*Graphics*), *call* repaint( )

**repaint( ):**

- Call repaint( ) when you have changed something and want your changes to show up on the screen
- You do *not* need to call repaint() when something in Java's own components

  (Buttons, TextFields, etc.)
- You *do* need to call repaint() after drawing commands (drawRect(...), fillRect(...), drawString(...), etc.)
- repaint( ) is a *request*--it might not happen
- When you call repaint( ), Java schedules a call to update(Graphics g)

**update( )**

- When you call repaint( ), Java schedules a call to update(Graphics g)
- Here's what update does:

```
public void update(Graphics g) {
// Fills applet with background color, then
paint(g);
}
```

### *Simple Example of Applet by Applet Viewer Tool*

- To execute the applet by appletviewer tool, create an applet that contains applet tag in comment and compile it. After that run it by: appletviewer First.java. Now Html file is not required but it is for testing purpose only.

```
//First.java
        import java.applet.Applet; import
        java.awt.Graphics; public class
        First extends Applet{
        public void paint(Graphics g){
        g.drawString("welcome to applet",150,150);
}
}
/*
<applet code="First.class" width="300" height="300">
</applet> */
```

To execute the applet by appletviewer tool, write in command prompt:

```
c:\>javac First.java
c:\>appletviewer First.java
```

### *Displaying Graphics in Applet*

- java.awt.Graphics class provides many methods for graphics programming.

### *Commonly Used Methods of Graphics Class*

- **public abstract void drawString(String str, int x, int y):** is used to draw the specified string.
- **public void drawRect(int x, int y, int width, int height):** draws a rectangle with the specified width and height.
- **public abstract void fillRect(int x, int y, int width, int height):** is used to fill rectangle with the default color and specified width and height.
- **public abstract void drawOval(int x, int y, int width, int height):** is used to draw oval with the specified width and height.
- **public abstract void fillOval(int x, int y, int width, int height):** is used to fill oval with the default color and specified width and height.
- **public abstract void drawLine(int x1, int y1, int x2, int y2)**: is used to draw line between the points(x1, y1) and (x2, y2).

- **public abstract boolean drawImage(Image img, int x, int y, ImageObserver observer):** is used draw the specified image.
- **public abstract void drawArc(int x, int y, int width, int height, int startAngle, int arcAngle):** is used draw a circular or elliptical arc.
- **public abstract void fillArc(int x, int y, int width, int height, int startAngle, int arcAngle):** is used to fill a circular or elliptical arc.
- **public abstract void setColor(Color c):** is used to set the graphics current color to the specified color.
- **public abstract void setFont(Font font):** is used to set the graphics current font to the specified font.

### *Example of Graphics in Applet*

```
import java.applet.Applet;
import java.awt.*;
public class GraphicsDemo extends Applet{
public void paint(Graphics g){
g.setColor(Color.red);
g.drawString("Welcome",50, 50);
g.drawLine(20,30,20,300);
g.drawRect(70,100,30,30);
g.fillRect(170,100,30,30);
g.drawOval(70,200,30,30);
g.setColor(Color.pink);
g.fillOval(170,200,30,30);
g.drawArc(90,150,30,30,30,270);
g.fillArc(270,150,30,30,0,180);
}
}
myapplet.html
<html>
<body>
<applet code="GraphicsDemo.class" width="300" height="300">
</applet>
</body>
</html>
```

### *Two Types of Applets*

- It is important to state at the outset that there are two varieties of applets. The first are those based directly on the Applet class described in this chapter. These applets use the Abstract Window Toolkit (AWT) to provide the graphic user interface (or use no GUI at all). This style of applet has been available since Java was first created.
- The second type of applets are those based on the Swing class JApplet. Swing applets use the Swing classes to provide the GUI. Swing offers a richer and often easier-to-use user interface than does the AWT. Thus, Swing-based applets are now the most popular. However, traditional AWT-based applets are still used, especially when only a very simple user interface is required.

Thus, both AWT- and Swing-based applets are valid.

- Because JApplet inherits Applet, all the features of Applet are also available in JApplet, and most of the information in this chapter applies to both types of applets. Therefore, even if you are interested in only Swing applets, the information in this chapter is still relevant and necessary. Understand, however, that when creating Swing-based applets, some additional constraints apply and these are described later in this topic, when Swing is covered

## 5.4. Event Handling

- For the user to interact with a GUI, the underlying operating system must support event handling.
- Operating systems constantly monitor events such as keystrokes, mouse clicks, voice command, etc.
- operating systems sort out these events and report them to the appropriate application programs each application program then decides what to do in response to these events

### *Events*

- An event is an object that describes a state change in a source.
- It can be generated as a consequence of a person interacting with the elements in a graphical user interface.
- Some of the activities that cause events to be generated are pressing a button, entering a character via the keyboard, selecting an item in a list, and clicking the mouse.

- Events may also occur that are not directly caused by interactions with a user interface.
- For example, an event may be generated when a timer expires, a counter exceeds a value, a software or hardware failure occurs, or an operation is completed.
- Events can be defined as needed and appropriate by application.

### *Event Sources*

- A source is an object that generates an event.
- This occurs when the internal state of that object changes in some way.
- Sources may generate more than one type of event.
- Source must register listeners in order for the listeners to receive notifications about a specific type of event.
- Each type of event has its own registration method.
- General form is:
- public void addTypeListener(TypeListener el)

Here, Type is the name of the event and el is a reference to the event listener. For example,

- The method that registers a keyboard event listener is called addKeyListener ().
- The method that registers a mouse motion listener is called addMouseMotionListener ( ).
- When an event occurs, all registered listeners are notified and receive a copy of the event object. This is known as multicasting the event.
- In all cases, notifications are sent only to listeners that register to receive them.
- Some sources may allow only one listener to register. The general form is:
    - public void addTypeListener(TypeListener el) throws java.util.TooManyListenersException

      Here Type is the name of the event and el is a reference to the event listener.
- When such an event occurs, the registered listener is notified. This is known as unicasting the event.
- A source must also provide a method that allows a listener to unregister an interest in a specific type of event.
- The general form is:
    - public void removeTypeListener(TypeListener el)

Here, Type is the name of the event and el is a reference to the event listener.

- For example, to remove a keyboard listener, you would call removeKeyListener( ).

- The methods that add or remove listeners are provided by the source that generates events.

- For example, the Component class provides methods to add and remove keyboard and mouse event listeners.

### *Event Classes*

- The Event classes that represent events are at the core of Java's event handling mechanism.
- Super class of the Java event class hierarchy is EventObject, which is in java.util. for all events.
- Constructor is :
    - EventObject(Object src)
        - Here, src is the object that generates this event.
- EventObject contains two methods: getSource( ) and toString( ).
    - The getSource( ) method returns the source of the event. General form is : Object getSource( )
    - The toString( ) returns the string equivalent of the event.
- EventObject is a superclass of all events.
- AWTEvent is a superclass of all AWT events that are handled by the delegation event model.
- The package java.awt.event defines several types of events that are generated by various user interface elements.
- Event Classes in java.awt.event
    - ActionEvent: Generated when a button is pressed, a list item is double clicked, or a menu item is selected.
    - AdjustmentEvent: Generated when a scroll bar is manipulated.
    - ComponentEvent: Generated when a component is hidden, moved, resized, or becomes visible.
    - ContainerEvent: Generated when a component is added to or removed from a container.
    - FocusEvent: Generated when a component gains or loses keyboard focus.
    - InputEvent: Abstract super class for all component input event classes.
    - ItemEvent: Generated when a check box or list item is clicked also occurs when a choice selection is made or a checkable menu item is selected or deselected.

- KeyEvent: Generated when input is received from the keyboard.
- MouseEvent: Generated when the mouse is dragged, moved, clicked, pressed, or released; also generated when the mouse enters or exits a component.
- TextEvent: Generated when the value of a text area or text field is changed.
- WindowEvent: Generated when a window is activated, closed, deactivated, deiconified, iconified, opened, or quit.

## 5.5. Event Listeners

- A listener is an object that is notified when an event occurs.
- Event has two major requirements.
    - It must have been registered with one or more sources to receive notifications about specific types of events.
    - It must implement methods to receive and process these notifications.
- The methods that receive and process events are defined in a set of interfaces found in java.awt.event.
- For example, the MouseMotionListener interface defines two methods to receive notifications when the mouse is dragged or moved.
- Any object may receive and process one or both of these events if it provides an implementation of this interface.

## 5.6. Delegation Event Model

- The modern approach to handling events is based on the delegation event model, which defines standard and consistent mechanisms to generate and process events.
- Its concept is quite simple: a source generates an event and sends it to one or more listeners.
- In this scheme, the listener simply waits until it receives an event.
- Once received, the listener processes the event and then returns.
- The advantage of this design is that the application logic that processes events is cleanly separated from the user interface logic that generates those events.
- A user interface element is able to "delegate" the processing of an event to a separate piece of code.
- In the delegation event model, listeners must register with a source in order to receive an event notification. This provides an important benefit: notifications are sent only to listeners that want to receive them.

- This is a more efficient way to handle events than the design used by the old Java 1.0 approach. Previously, an event was propagated up the containment hierarchy until it was handled by a component.
- This required components to receive events that they did not process, and it wasted valuable time. The delegation event model eliminates this overhead.
- Note:
    - Java also allows you to process events without using the delegation event model.
    - This can be done by extending an AWT component.

### *Handling Mouse Events*

- mouse events can be handled by implementing the MouseListener and the MouseMotionListener interfaces.
- MouseListener Interface defines five methods. The general forms of these methods are:
    - void mouseClicked(MouseEvent me)
    - void mouseEntered(MouseEvent me)
    - void mouseExited(MouseEvent me)
    - void mousePressed(MouseEvent me)
    - void mouseReleased(MouseEvent me)
- MouseMotionListener Interface. This interface defines two methods. Their general forms are:
    - void mouseDragged(MouseEvent me)
    - void mouseMoved(MouseEvent me)

### *Handling Keyboard Events*

- Keyboard events, can be handled by implementing the **KeyListener** interface.
- **KeyListner** interface defines three methods. The general forms of these methods are :
    - void keyPressed(KeyEvent ke)
    - void keyReleased(KeyEvent ke)
    - void keyTyped(KeyEvent ke)
- To implement keyboard events implementation to the above methods is needed.

### *Adapter Classes*

- Java provides a special feature, called an adapter class that can simplify the creation of event handlers.

- An adapter class provides an empty implementation of all methods in an event listener interface.
- Adapter classes are useful when you want to receive and process only some of the events that are handled by a particular event listener interface.
- You can define a new class to act as an event listener by extending one of the adapter classes and implementing only those events in which you are interested.
- Adapter classes in java.awt.event are.

| Adapter Class | Listener Interface |
|---|---|
| ComponentAdapter | ComponentListener |
| ContainerAdapter | ContainerListener |
| FocusAdapter | FocusListener |
| KeyAdapter | KeyListener |
| MouseAdapter | MouseListener |
| MouseMotionAdapter | MouseMotionListener |
| WindowAdapter | WindowListener |

***Inner Classes***

- Inner classes, which allow one class to be defined within another.
- An inner class is a non-static nested class. It has access to all of the variables and methods of its outer class and may refer to them directly in the same way that other non-static members of the outer class do.
- An inner class is fully within the scope of its enclosing class.
- An inner class has access to all of the members of its enclosing class, but the reverse is not true.
- Members of the inner class are known only within the scope of the inner class and may not be used by the outer class

## 5.7. The AWT Class Hierarchy

- The AWT classes are contained in the java.awt package. It is one of Java's largest packages. some of the AWT classes.
- AWT Classes
  - AWTEvent:Encapsulates AWT events.
  - AWTEventMulticaster: Dispatches events to multiple listeners.

- BorderLayout: The border layout manager. Border layouts use five components: North, South, East, West, and Center.
- Button: Creates a push button control.
- Canvas: A blank, semantics-free window.
- CardLayout: The card layout manager. Card layouts emulate index cards. Only the one on top is showing.
- Checkbox: Creates a check box control.
- CheckboxGroup: Creates a group of check box controls.
- CheckboxMenuItem: Creates an on/off menu item.
- Choice: Creates a pop-up list.
- Color: Manages colors in a portable, platform-independent fashion.
- Component: An abstract super class for various AWT components.
- Container: A subclass of Component that can hold other components.
- Cursor: Encapsulates a bitmapped cursor.
- Dialog: Creates a dialog window.
- Dimension: Specifies the dimensions of an object. The width is stored in width, and the height is stored in height.
- Event: Encapsulates events.
- EventQueue: Queues events.
- FileDialog: Creates a window from which a file can be selected.
- FlowLayout: The flow layout manager. Flow layout positions components left to right, top to bottom.
- Font: Encapsulates a type font.
- FontMetrics: Encapsulates various information related to a font. This information helps you display text in a window.
- Frame: Creates a standard window that has a title bar, resize corners, and a menu bar.
- Graphics: Encapsulates the graphics context. This context is used by various output methods to display output in a window.
- GraphicsDevice: Describes a graphics device such as a screen or printer.
- GraphicsEnvironment: Describes the collection of available Font and GraphicsDevice objects.
- GridBagConstraints: Defines various constraints relating to the GridBagLayout class.

- GridBagLayout: The grid bag layout manager. Grid bag layout displays components subject to the constraints specified by GridBagConstraints.
- GridLayout: The grid layout manager. Grid layout displays components i n a two-dimensional grid.
- Scrollbar: Creates a scroll bar control.
- ScrollPane: A container that provides horizontal and/or vertical scrollbars for another component.
- SystemColor: Contains the colors of GUI widgets such as windows, scrollbars, text, and others.
- TextArea: Creates a multiline edit control.
- TextComponent: A super class for TextArea and TextField.
- TextField: Creates a single-line edit control.
- Toolkit: Abstract class implemented by the AWT.
- Window: Creates a window with no frame, no menu bar, and no title.

## 5.8. User Interface Components

### *Labels*

- Creates a label that displays a string.
- A label is an object of type Label, and it contains a string, which it displays.
- Labels are passive controls that do not support any interaction with the user.
- Label defines the following constructors:
    - Label( )-- creates a blank label.
    - Label(String str)-- creates a label that contains the string specified by str. This string is left-justified
    - Label (String str, int how) -- creates a label that contains the string specified by str using the alignment specified by how.
        - The value of how must be one of these three constants:
        - Label.LEFT, Label.RIGHT, or Label.CENTER
- methods are shown here:
    - void setText(String str)-- specifies the new label
    - String getText( )- -the current label is returned.
    - void setAlignment(int how) set the alignment of the string within the label
    - int getAlignment( )-- obtain the current alignment

- Label creation: Label one = new Label("One");

### *Button*

- The most widely used control is the push button.
- A push button is a component that contains a label and that generates an event when it is pressed.
- Push buttons are objects of type Button. Button defines these two constructors:
- Button( )-- creates an empty button
- Button(String str)-- creates a button that contains str as a label
- methods are as follows:
    - void setLabel(String str)-- set its new label
    - String getLabel( )-- retrieve its label
- Button creation: Button yes = new Button("Yes");

### *Canvas*

- It is not part of the hierarchy for applet or frame windows
- Canvas encapsulates a blank window upon which you can draw.
- Canvas creation:
    - Canvas c = new Canvas();
- Image test = c.createImage(200, 100);-- to actually make an Image object. that image is blank.

### *Scrollbars*

- Scrollbar generates adjustment events when the scroll bar is manipulated.
- Scrollbar creates a scroll bar control.
- Scroll bars are used to select continuous values between a specified minimum and maximum.
- Scroll bars may be oriented horizontally or vertically.
- A scroll bar is actually a composite of several individual parts.
- Each end has an arrow that you can click to move the current value of the scroll bar one unit in the direction of the arrow.
- The current value of the scroll bar relative to its minimum and maximum values is indicated by the slider box (or thumb) for the scroll bar.
- The slider box can be dragged by the user to a new position. The scroll bar will then reflect this value.

- Scrollbar defines the following constructors:
  - Scrollbar( )-- creates a vertical scroll bar
  - Scrollbar(int style)-- to specify the orientation of the scroll bar.
  - Scrollbar(int style, int initialValue, int thumbSize, int min, int max)-- to specify the orientation of the scroll bar.
    - If style is Scrollbar.VERTICAL, a vertical scroll bar is created.
    - If style is Scrollbar.HORIZONTAL, the scroll bar is horizontal
    - The initial value of the scroll bar is passed in initialValue.
    - The number of units represented by the height of the thumb is passed in thumbSize.
    - The minimum and maximum values for the scroll bar are specified by min and max.
- vertSB = new Scrollbar(Scrollbar.VERTICAL, 0, 1, 0, height);
- horzSB = new Scrollbar(Scrollbar.HORIZONTAL, 0, 1, 0, width);

### *Text*

- Text is created by Using a TextField class
- The TextField class implements a single-line text-entry area, usually called an edit control.
- Text fields allow the user to enter strings and to edit the text using the arrow keys, cut and paste keys, and mouse selections.
- TextField is a subclass of TextComponent.
- TextField defines the following constructors:
  - TextField( )-- creates a default text field.
  - TextField(int numChars)-- creates a text field that is numChars characters wide.
  - TextField(String str)- form initializes the text field with the string contained in str.
  - TextField(String str, int numChars)- initializes a text field and sets its width.
- Methods
  - String getText( )- obtain the string currently contained in the text field
  - void setText(String str)- To set the text. str is the new string.

### *Components*

- At the top of the AWT hierarchy is the Component class.

- Component is an abstract class that encapsulates all of the attributes of a visual component.
- All user interface elements that are displayed on the screen and that interact with the user are subclasses of Component.
- It defines public methods that are responsible for managing events, such as mouse and keyboard input, positioning and sizing the window, and repainting.
- A Component object is responsible for remembering the current foreground and background colors and the currently selected text font.
- Component add(Component compObj) -- To add components
  - Here, *compObj* is an instance of the control that you want to add.
  - A reference to *compObj* is returned.
- Once a control has been added, it will automatically be visible whenever its parent window is displayed.
- void remove(Component obj) -To remove a control from a window when the control is no longer needed
  - Here, *obj* is a reference to the control you want to remove.
  - You can remove all controls by calling **removeAll( )**.

### *Check Box*

- A check box is a control that is used to turn an option on or off. It consists of a small box that can either contain a check mark or not.
- There is a label associated with each check box that describes what option the box represents.
- You can change the state of a check box by clicking on it.
- Check boxes can be used individually or as part of a group.
- Checkboxes are objects of the Checkbox class.
- Checkbox supports these constructors:
  - Checkbox( )-
    - Creates a check box whose label is initially blank.
    - The state of the check box is unchecked.
      - Checkbox(String str)- creates a check box whose label is specified by str. The state of the check
      - Checkbox(String str, boolean on)-
  - Allows you to set the initial state of the check box.

- If on is true, the check box is initially checked; otherwise, it is cleared.
    - Checkbox(String str, boolean on, CheckboxGroup cbGroup)
    - Checkbox(String str, CheckboxGroup cbGroup, boolean on)
  - whose label is specified by str and
  - whose group is specified by cbGroup. If this check box is not part of a group, then cbGroup must be null.
  - The value of on determines the initial state of the check box.
- methods are as follows:
  - boolean getState( )- To retrieve the current state of a check box
  - void setState(boolean on)- To set its state
  - Here, if on is true, the box is checked. If it is false, the box is cleared.
  - String getLabel( )-- To retrieve the current label
  - void setLabel(String str)-- To set the label
- Checkbox creation:
  - CheckBox Win98 = new Checkbox("Windows 98", null, true);

### *Check Box Groups*

- It is possible to create a set of mutually exclusive check boxes in which one and only one check box in the group can be checked at any one time.
- These check boxes are often called radio buttons.
- To create a set of mutually exclusive check boxes, you must first define the group to which they will belong and then specify that group when you construct the check boxes.
- Check box groups are objects of type CheckboxGroup. Only the default constructor is defined, which creates an empty group.
- methods
  - Checkbox getSelectedCheckbox( ) - determine which check box in a group is currently selected
  - void setSelectedCheckbox(Checkbox which) - set a check box
    - Here, which is the check box that you want to be selected.
    - The previously selected checkbox will be turned off.
- CheckboxGroup cbg = new CheckboxGroup();
- Win98 = new Checkbox("Windows 98", cbg, true);
- winNT = new Checkbox("Windows NT", cbg, false);

### *Choices*

- The Choice class is used to create a pop-up list of items from which the user may choose.
- A Choice control is a form of menu.
- Choice only defines the default constructor, which creates an empty list.
- Methods:
  - void addItem(String name)- add a selection to the list
  - void add(String name)- add a selection to the list
  - Here, name is the name of the item being added.
  - String getSelectedItem( )- determine which item is currently selected,
  - int getSelectedIndex( ) determine which item is currently selected,

### *Lists*

- The List class provides a compact, multiple-choice, scrolling selection list.
- List object can be constructed to show any number of choices in the visible window.
- It can also be created to allow multiple selections.
- List provides these constructors:
  - List( )
  - List(int numRows)
  - List(int numRows, boolean multipleSelect)
- Methods
  - void add(String name) - add a selection to the list
  - void add(String name, int index) - add a selection to the list
  - Ex: List os = new List(4, true);

### *Panels*

- Panel is a window that does not contain a title bar, menu bar, or border.
- The Panel class is a concrete subclass of Container.
- It doesn't add any new methods; it simply implements Container.
- A Panel may be thought of as a recursively nestable, concrete screen component.
- Panel is the superclass for Applet.
- Methods
- When screen output is directed to an applet, it is drawn on the surface of a Panel object.

- Methods(inherited)
    - add( ) --Components can be added to a Panel object.
    - setLocation( ), setSize( ), or setBounds( )-- position and resize them
- Ex: Panel osCards = new Panel();
- CardLayout cardLO = new CardLayout();
- osCards.setLayout(cardLO);
- A scroll pane is a component that presents a rectangular area in which a component may be viewed.
- Horizontal and/or vertical scroll bars may be provided if necessary.
- Constants are defined by the ScrollPaneConstants interface.
    - HORIZONTAL_SCROLLBAR_ALWAYS
    - HORIZONTAL_SCROLLBAR_AS_NEEDED
    - VERTICAL_SCROLLBAR_ALWAYS
    - VERTICAL_SCROLLBAR_AS_NEEDED

### *Dialogs*

- Dialog class creates a dialog window.
- constructors are :
    - Dialog(Frame parentWindow, boolean mode)
    - Dialog(Frame parentWindow, String title, boolean mode)
- The dialog box allows you to choose a method that should be invoked when the button is clicked.
- Ex: Font f = new Font("Dialog", Font.PLAIN, 12);

### *Menu Bar*

- Menu Bar class creates a menu bar.
- A top-level window can have a menu bar associated with it. A menu bar displays a list of top-level menu choices. Each choice is associated with a drop-down menu.
- To create a menu bar, first create an instance of Menu Bar. By its default constructor.
- Create instances of Menu that will define the selections displayed on the bar.
- Following are the constructors for Menu:
    - Menu( )
    - Menu(String optionName)
    - Menu(String optionName, boolean removable)

- Methods
  - MenuItem add(MenuItem item) -- add the item to a Menu
  - Here, item is the item being added. Items are added to a menu in the order in which the calls to add( ) take place.
  - Menu add(Menu menu) -- add menu object to the menu bar

### *Graphics*

- The AWT supports a rich assortment of graphics methods.
- All graphics are drawn relative to a window.
- A graphics context is encapsulated by the Graphics class
- It is passed to an applet when one of its various methods, such as paint( ) or update( ), is called.
- It is returned by the getGraphics( ) method of Component.
- The Graphics class defines a number of drawing functions. Each shape can be drawn edge-only or filled.
- Objects are drawn and filled in the currently selected graphics color, which is black by default.
- When a graphics object is drawn that exceeds the dimensions of the window, output is automatically clipped
- Ex:

```
Public void paint(Graphics g)
{
G.drawString("welcome",20,20);
}
```

## 5.9. Layout Manager

- A layout manager automatically arranges your controls within a window by using some type of algorithm.
- It is very tedious to manually lay out a large number of components and sometimes the width and height information is not yet available when you need to arrange some control, because the native toolkit components haven't been realized.
- Each **Container** object has a layout manager associated with it.
- A layout manager is an instance of any class that implements the **LayoutManager** interface.

- The layout manager is set by the **setLayout( )** method. If no call to **setLayout ( )** is made, then the default layout manager is used.
- Whenever a container is resized (or sized for the first time), the layout manager is used to position each of the components within it.
- Different types of layout managers
    - Border Layout
    - Grid Layout
    - Flow Layout
    - Card Layout
    - GridBag Layout

### *Border Layout*

- The **BorderLayout** class implements a common layout style for top-level windows. It has four narrow, fixed-width components at the edges and one large area in the center.
- The four sides are referred to as north, south, east, and west. The middle area is called the center.
- The constructors defined by **BorderLayout**:
    - BorderLayout( )
    - BorderLayout(int horz, int vert)
- **BorderLayout** defines the following constants that specify the regions:
    - BorderLayout.CENTER
    - B orderLayout.SOUTH
    - BorderLayout. EAST
    - BorderLayout.WEST
    - BorderLayout. NORTH
- void add(Component compObj, Object region)—to add the components

### *Grid Layout*

- **GridLayout** lays out components in a two-dimensional grid. When you instantiate a
- **GridLayout**, you define the number of rows and columns.
- The constructors are
    - GridLayout( ) - creates a single-column grid layout.

- GridLayout(int numRows, int numColumns )- creates a grid layout with the specified number of rows and columns
- GridLayout(int numRows, int numColumns, int horz, int vert)
    - *horz* and *vert*, specifies the horizontal and vertical space left between components.
    - Either *numRows* or *numColumns* can be zero. Specifying *numRows* as zero allows for unlimited-length columns. Specifying *numColumns* as zero allows for unlimited-lengthrows.

### *Flow Layout*

- **FlowLayout** is the default layout manager.
- Components are laid out from the upper-left corner, left to right and top to bottom. When no more components fit on a line, the next one appears on the next line. A small space is left between each component, above and below, as well as left and right.
- The constructors are
- FlowLayout( ) - creates the default layout, which centers components and leaves five pixels of space between each component.
- FlowLayout(int *how)* –
    - *how* specifies that how each line is aligned.
    - Valid values for *how* are:
        - FlowLayout.LEFT
        - FlowLayout.CENTER
        - FlowLayout.RIGHT
- FlowLayout(int *how,* int *horz,* int *vert*)-specifies the horizontal and vertical space left between components in *horz* and *vert,* respectively

### *Card Layout*

- The **CardLayout** class is unique among the other layout managers in that it stores several different layouts.
- Each layout can be thought of as being on a separate index card in a deck that can be shuffled so that any card is on top at a given time.
- **CardLayout** provides these two constructors:
    - CardLayout( )
    - CardLayout(int horz, int vert)

- The cards are held in an object of type **Panel**. This panel must have **CardLayout** selected as its layout manager.
- void add(Component panelObj, Object name); -- Cards are added to panel
- methods defined by **CardLayout**:
    - void first(Container deck)
    - void last(Container deck)
    - void next(Container deck)
    - void previous(Container deck)
    - void show(Container deck, String cardName)

### *GridBag Layout*

- The Grid bag layout displays components subject to the constraints specified by GridBagConstraints.
- **GridLayout** lays out components in a two-dimensional grid.
- The constructors are
    - GridLayout( )
    - GridLayout(int numRows, int numColumns )
    - GridLayout(int numRows, int numColumns, int horz, int vert)

# CHAPTER VI

# AWT

## 6.1. Java AWT

- Java AWT (Abstract Windowing Toolkit) is an API to develop GUI or window-based application in java.
- Java AWT components are platform-dependent i.e. components are displayed according to the view of operating system. AWT is heavyweight i.e. its components uses the resources of system.
- The java.awt package provides classes for AWT api such as TextField, Label, TextArea, RadioButton, CheckBox, Choice, List etc.

## 6.2. Java AWT Hierarchy

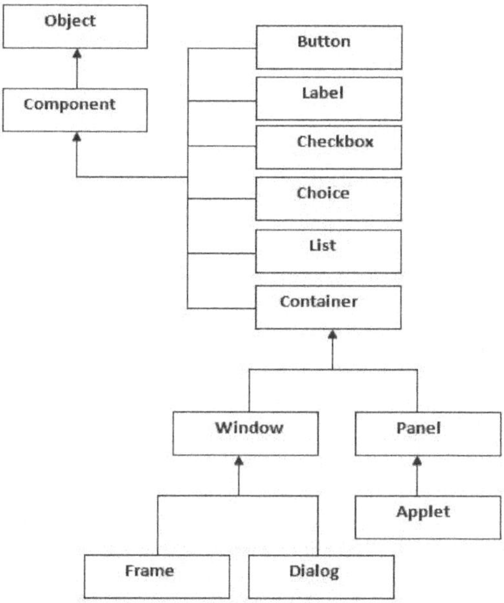


- The hierarchy of Java AWT classes are given below.

## 6.3. Container Classes

- These are the predefined classes in java.awt package which can be used to display all non-container classes to the end user in the frame of window. container classes are; frame, panel.

## 6.4. Non-container Classes

- These are the predefined classes used to design the input field so that end user can provide input value to communicate with java program, these are also treated as GUI component. non-container classes are; Label, Button, List etc...

### *Non-container Classes*

- These are the predefined classes used to design the input field so that end user can provide input value to communicate with java program, these are also treated as GUI component.

### *Label*

It can be any user defined name used to identify input field like textbox, textarea etc.

### *Example*

**Label l1=new**

**Label("uname"); Label**

**l2=new**

**Label("password");**

### *TextField*

This class can be used to design textbox.

**Example**

**TextField**

**tf=new**

**TextField();**

**Example**

**TextField tf=new**

**TextField(40);**

### *Button*

This class can be used to create a push button.

**Example**

**Button b1=new Button("submit");**

**Button b2=new**

**Button("cancel"); TextArea**

This class can be used to design a textarea, which will accept number of characters in rows and columns formate.

***Example***

```
TextArea ta=new TextArea(5, 10);
```

// here 5 is no. of rows and 10 is no. of column

Note: In above example at a time we can give the contains in textarea is in 5 rows and 9 column (n-1 columns).

***Checkbox***

This class can be used to design multi selection checkbox.

***Example***

```
Checkbox cb1=new
 Checkbox(".net");
Checkbox cb2=new
 Checkbox("Java");
Checkbox cb3=new
Checkbox("html");
Checkbox cb4=new
 Checkbox("php");
```

***CheckboxGroup***

This class can be used to design radio button. Radio button is used for single selection.

***Example***

```
CheckboxGroup cbg=new
CheckboxGroup(); Checkbox cb=new
Checkbox("male", cbg, "true"); Checkbox
cb=new Checkbox("female", cbg, "false");
```

Note: Under one group many number of radio button can exist but only one can be selected at a time.

***Choice***

This class can be used to design a drop down box with more options and supports single selection.

***Example***

```
Choice c=new Choice();
```

c.add(20);

c.add(21);

c.add(22);

dd(23);

### *List*

This class can be used to design a list box with multiple options and support multi selection.

**Example**

**List l=new List(3); l.add("goa");**

**l.add("delhi");**

**l.add("pune");**

Note: By holding clt button multiple options can be selected.

### *Scrollbar*

This class can be used to display a scroolbar on the window.

### *Example*

**Scrollbar sb=new Scrollbar(type of scrollbar, initialposition, thamb width, minmum value, maximum value);**

Initial position represent very starting point or position of thumb. Thumb width represent the size of thumb which is scroll on scrollbar Minimum and maxium value represent boundries of scrollbar

### *Type of Scrollbar*

There are two types of scrollbar are available;

**scrollbar.vertical**

**scrollbar.horizental**

### *Example*

**Scrollbar sb=new Scrollbar(Scrollbar.HORIZENTAL, 10, 5, 0, 100);**

## 6.5. AWT Frame

***Frame***

It is a predefined class used to create a container with the title bar and body part.

***Example***

**Frame f=new**

**Frame(); Mostly**

**used methods**

**setTitle()**

It is used to display user defined message on title bar.

***Example***

**Frame f=new Frame();**

**f.setTitle("myframe");**

**setBackground()**

It is used to set background or image of frame.

***Example***

**Frame f=new Frame();**

**f.setBackground(Color.red);**

**Example**

**Frame f=new Frame();**

**f.setBackground("c:\image\myimage.png");**

**setForground()**

It is used to set the foreground text color.

***Example***

**Frame f=new Frame(); f.setForground(Color.red);**

**setSize()**

It is used to set the width and height for frame.

**setVisible()**

**Example**

**Frame f=new**

**Frame();**

**f.setSize(400,300);**

It is used to make the frame as visible to end user.

***Example***

**Frame f=new Frame(); f.setVisible(true);**

Note: You can write setVisible(true) or setVisible(false), if it is true then it visible otherwise not visible.

**setLayout()**

It is used to set any layout to the frame. You can also set null layout it means no any layout apply on frame.

***Example***

**Frame f=new Frame(); f.setLayout(new FlowLayout());**

Note: Layout is a logical container used to arrange the gui components in a specific order

**add()**

It is used to add non-container components (Button, List) to the frame.

***Example***

```
Frame f=new Frame();
Button b=new Button("Click"); f.add(b);
```

**Explanation**: In above code we add button on frame using f.add(b), here b is the object of Button class..

***Example of Frame***

```
import java.awt.*;
class FrameDemo
{
public static void main(String[] args)
{
Frame f=new Frame();
f.setTitle("myframe");
```

```
f.setBackground(Color.cyan);
f.setForeground(Color.red);
f.setLayout(new FlowLayout());
Button b1=new Button("Submit");
Button b2=new Button("Cancel"); f.add(b1);
f.add(b2);
f.setSize(500,300);
f.setVisible(true);
}
}
```

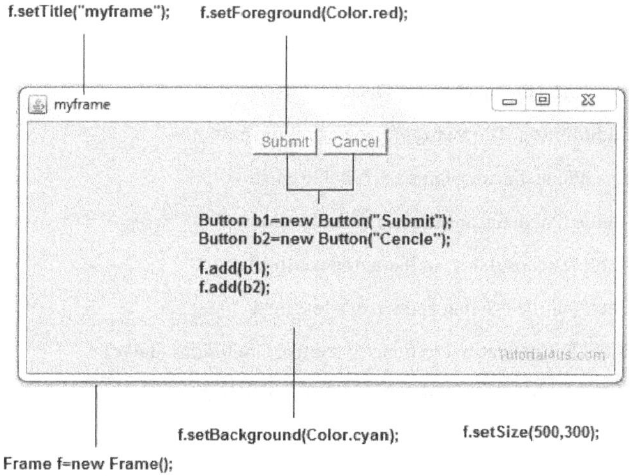


## 6.6. Introduction to Swings

- Swing is a set of classes that provides more powerful and flexible components than are possible with the AWT.
- In addition to the familiar components, such as buttons, checkboxes, and labels, Swing supplies several exciting additions, including tabbed panes, scroll panes, trees, and tables.
- Even familiar components such as buttons have more capabilities in Swing.
- For example, a button may have both an image and a text string associated with it. Also, the image can be changed as the state of the button changes.
- Unlike AWT components, Swing components are not implemented by platform- specific code.

- Instead, they are written entirely in Java and, therefore, are platform-independent.
- The term lightweight is used to describe such elements The Swing component are defined in javax.swing
    - AbstractButton: Abstract superclass for Swing buttons.
    - ButtonGroup: Encapsulates a mutually exclusive set of buttons.
    - ImageIcon: Encapsulates an icon.
    - JApplet: The Swing version of Applet.
    - JButton: The Swing push button class.
    - JCheckBox: The Swing check box class.
    - JComboBox : Encapsulates a combo box (an combination of a drop-down list and text field).
    - JLabel: The Swing version of a label.
    - JRadioButton: The Swing version of a radio button.
    - JScrollPane: Encapsulates a scrollable window.
    - JTabbedPane: Encapsulates a tabbed window.
    - JTable: Encapsulates a table-based control.
    - JTextField: The Swing version of a text field.
    - JTree: Encapsulates a tree-based control Limitations of AWT
    - AWT supports limited number of GUI components.
    - AWT components are heavy weight components.
    - AWT components are developed by using platform specific code.
    - AWT components behaves differently in different operating systems.
    - AWT component is converted by the native code of the operating system.
    - Lowest Common Denominator
        - If not available natively on one Java platform, not available on any Java platform
    - Simple Component Set
    - Components Peer-Based
        - Platform controls component appearance
        - Inconsistencies in implementations
    - Interfacing to native platform error-prone

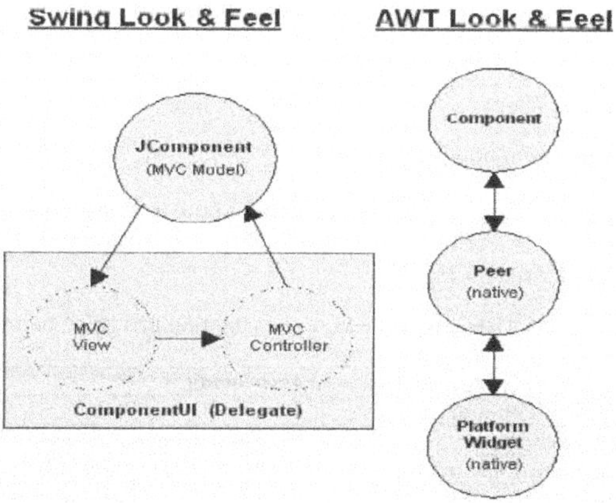


MODEL VIEW CONTROLLER ARCHITECTURE

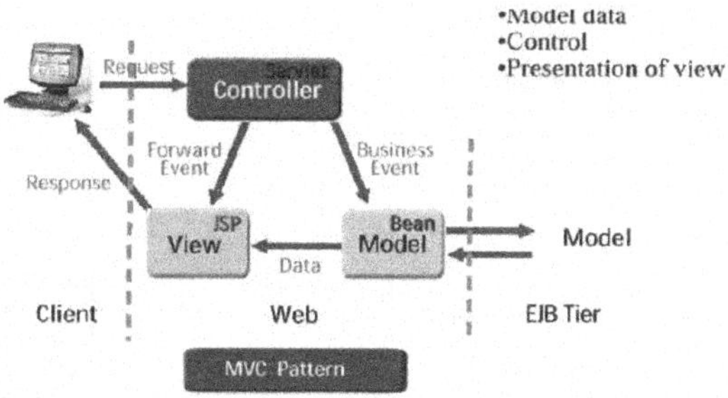


### *Model*

- Model consists of data and the functions that operate on data
- Java bean that we use to store data is a model component
- EJB can also be used as a model component

### *View*

- View is the front end that user interact.
- View can be a
  - HTML
  - JSP
  - Struts ActionForm

## 6.7. Controller

Controller component responsibilities

- Receive request from client
- Map request to specific business operation
- Determine the view to display based on the result of the business operation

### *Difference between AWT and Swing*

There are many differences between java awt and swing that are given below.

| Java AWT | Java Swing |
|---|---|
| AWT components are **platform-dependent**. | |
| AWT components are **heavyweight**. | Swing components are **lightweight**. |
| AWT **doesn't support pluggable look and feel**. | Swing **supports pluggable look and feel**. |
| AWT provides **less components** than Swing. | Swing provides **more powerful components** such as tables, lists, scrollpanes, colorchooser, tabbedpane etc. |
| AWT **doesn't follows MVC**(Model View Controller) where model represents data, view represents presentation and controller acts as an interface between model and view. | Swing **follows MVC**. |

### *Hierarchy of Swings*

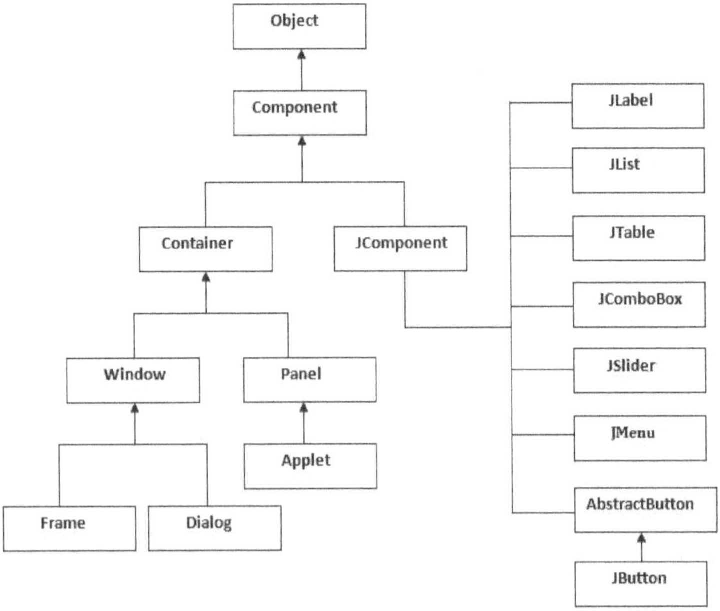


The methods of Component class are widely used in java swing that are given below.

| Method | Description |
|---|---|
| public void add(Component c) | add a component on another component. |
| public void setSize(int width,int height) | sets size of the component. |
| public void setLayout(LayoutManager m) | sets the layout manager for the component. |
| public void setVisible(boolean b) | sets the visibility of the component. It is by default false. |

### *Java Swing Examples*

There are two ways to create a frame:

- By creating the object of Frame class (association)
- By extending Frame class (inheritance)

We can write the code of swing inside

- The main()
- Constructor or any other method.

### *Simple Java Swing Example in main () method*

Let's see a simple swing example where we are creating one button and adding it on the JFrame object inside the main () method.

```
import javax.swing.*;
public class
FirstSwingExample { public
static void main(String[]
args) { JFrame f=new
JFrame();
JButton b=new JButton("click");//creating instance of JButton
b.setBounds(130,100,100, 40);//x axis, y axis, width, height
f.add(b);
    etSize(400,500);//400 width and
500 height f.setLayout(null);//using no
layout managers
f.setVisible(true);//making the frame
visible
  }
  }
```

### *Example of Swing by Association Inside Constructor*

We can also write all the codes of creating JFrame, JButton and method call inside the java constructor.

```
import javax.swing.*;
public class Simple {
JFrame f;
Simple(){
f=new JFrame();
JButton b=new JButton("click");
b.setBounds(130,100,100, 40);
f.add(b);
f.setSize(400,500);//400 width and 500 height
f.setLayout(null);
f.setVisible(true);
}
public static void main(String[] args) { new Simple();
}
}
```

### *Simple Example of Swing by Inheritance*

We can also inherit the JFrame class, so there is no need to create the instance of JFrame class explicitly.

```
import javax.swing.*;
public class Simple2 extends JFrame{
JFrame f;
Simple2(){
JButton b=new JButton("click");
b.setBounds(130,100,100, 40); add(b);
setSize(400,500);
setLayout(null);
setVisible(true);
}
public static void main(String[] args) { new
Simple2();
}
}
```

## 6.8. Components

- Container
  - JComponent
    - AbstractButton
  - JButton
  - JMenuItem
    - JCheckBoxMenuItem
    - JMenu
    - JRadioButtonMenuItem
  - JToggleButton
    - JCheckBox
    - JRadioButton
- JComponent
  - JTextComponent
  - JTextArea
  - JTextField
  - JPasswordField
  - JTextPane
  - JHTMLPane
- JComponent
- JTextComponent
  - JTextArea
  - JTextField
    - JPasswordField
  - JTextPane
    - JHTMLPane

***Containers***

- Top-Level Containers
- The components at the top of any Swing containment hierarchy

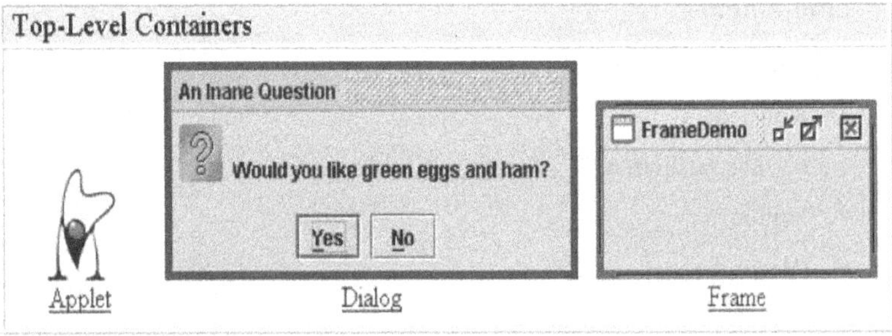


### *General Purpose Containers*

Intermediate containers that can be used under many different circumstances.

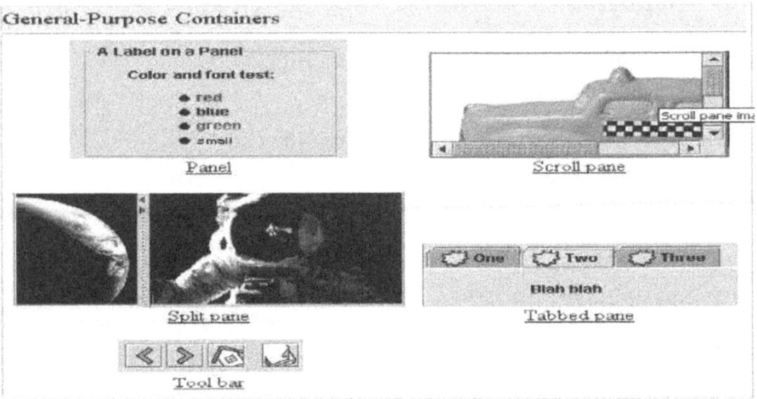


### *Special Purpose Container*

Intermediate containers that play specific roles in the UI.

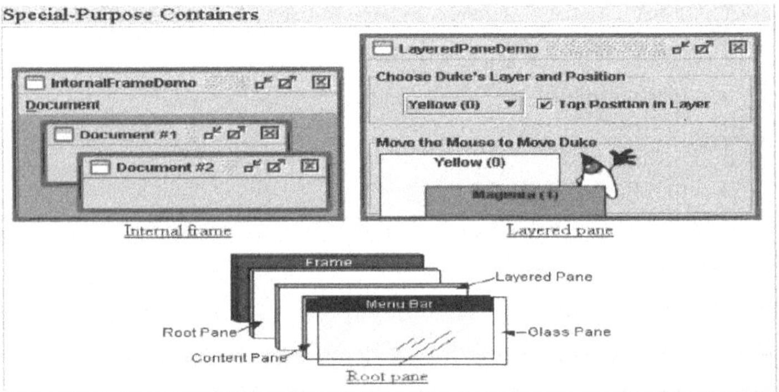

### *Exploring swing- JApplet*

If using Swing components in an applet, subclass JApplet, not Applet

- JApplet is a subclass of Applet
- Sets up special internal component event handling, among other things
- Can have a JMenuBar
- Default LayoutManager is BorderLayout

```
JFrame public class FrameTest { public
static void main (String args[]) {
JFrame f = new JFrame ("JFrame Example");
Container c = f.getContentPane();
c.setLayout (new FlowLayout()); for
(int i = 0; i < 5; i++) {
c.add (new JButton ("No"));
c.add (new Button ("Batter"));
}
c.add (new JLabel ("Swing"));
f.setSize (300, 200);
f.show();
}
}
```

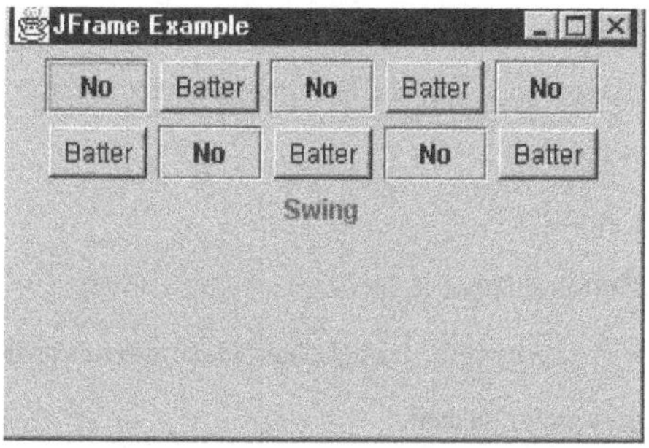


### *JComponent*

- JComponent supports the following components.
    - JComponent
        - JComboBox

        - JLabel
        - JList
        - JMenuBar
        - JPanel
        - JPopupMenu
        - JScrollBar
        - JScrollPane
        - JTextComponent
    - JTextArea
    - JTextField
        - JPasswordField
    - JTextPane
        - JHTMLPane

### *Icons and Labels*

- In Swing, icons are encapsulated by the ImageIcon class, which paints an icon from an image.
- constructors are:
    - ImageIcon(String filename)
    - ImageIcon(URL url)
- The ImageIcon class implements the Icon interface that declares the methods.
    - int getIconHeight( )
    - int getIconWidth( )
    - void paintIcon(Component comp,Graphics g,int x, int y)
- Swing labels are instances of the JLabel class, which extends JComponent.
- It can display text and/or an icon.
- Constructors are:
    - JLabel(Icon i)
    - Label(String s)
    - JLabel(String s, Icon i, int align)

- Here, s and i are the text and icon used for the label. The align argument is either LEFT, RIGHT, or CENTER. These constants are defined in the SwingConstants interface,
- Methods are:
  - Icon getIcon( )
  - String getText( )
  - void setIcon(Icon i)
  - void setText(String s)
    - Here, i and s are the icon and text, respectively.

### *Text Fields*

- The Swing text field is encapsulated by the JTextComponent class, which extendsJComponent.
- It provides functionality that is common to Swing text components.
- One of its subclasses is JTextField, which allows you to edit one line of text.
- Constructors are:
  - JTextField( )
  - JTextField(int cols)
  - JTextField(String s, int cols)
  - JTextField(String s)
    - Here, s is the string to be presented, and cols is the number of columns in the text field

### *Buttons*

- Swing buttons provide features that are not found in the Button class defined by the AWT.
- Swing buttons are subclasses of the AbstractButton class, which extends JComponent.
- AbstractButton contains many methods that allow you to control the behavior of buttons, check boxes, and radio buttons.
- Methods are:
  - void setDisabledIcon(Icon di)
  - void setPressedIcon(Icon pi)
  - void setSelectedIcon(Icon si)

- void setRolloverIcon(Icon ri)
    - Here, di, pi, si, and ri are the icons to be used for these different conditions.
- The text associated with a button can be read and written via the following methods:

### *JButton:::*

- String getText( )
- void setText(String s)
    - Here, s is the text to be associated with the button.
    - The JButton class provides the functionality of a push button.
- JButton allows an icon, a string, or both to be associated with the push button.
    - Some of its constructors are :
        - JButton(Icon i)
        - JButton(String s)
        - JButton(String s, Icon i)
            - Here, s and i are the string and icon used for the button.

### *Check Boxes*

- The JCheckBox class, which provides the functionality of a check box, is a concrete implementation of AbstractButton.
- Some of its constructors are shown here:
    - JCheckBox(Icon i)
    - JCheckBox(Icon i, boolean state)
    - JCheckBox(String s)
    - JCheckBox(String s, boolean state)
    - JCheckBox(String s, Icon i)
    - JCheckBox(String s, Icon i, boolean state)
        - Here, i is the icon for the button. The text is specified by s. If state is true, the check box is initially selected.
        - Otherwise, it is not.
- The state of the check box can be changed via the following method:
    - void setSelected(boolean state)

- Here, state is true if the check box should be checked.

### *Combo Boxes*

- Swing provides a *combo box* (a combination of a text field and a drop-down list) through the **JComboBox** class, which extends **JComponent**.
- A combo box normally displays one entry. However, it can also display a drop- down list that allows a user to select a different entry. You can also type your selection into the text field.
- Two of **JComboBox**'s constructors are :
  - JComboBox( )
  - JComboBox(Vector v)
    - Here, *v* is a vector that initializes the combo box.
  - Items are added to the list of choices via the **addItem( )** method, whose signature is:
  - void addItem(Object obj)
    - Here, *obj* is the object to be added to the combo box.

### *Radio Buttons*

- Radio buttons are supported by the JRadioButton class, which is a concrete implementation of AbstractButton.
- Some of its constructors are :
  - JRadioButton(Icon i)
  - JRadioButton(Icon i, boolean state)
  - JRadioButton(String s)
  - JRadioButton(String s, boolean state)
  - JRadioButton(String s, Icon i)
  - JRadioButton(String s, Icon i, boolean state)
    - Here, i is the icon for the button.
    - the text is specified by s.
    - If state is true, the button is initially selected.
    - Otherwise, it is not.
- Elements are then added to the button group via the following method:

- void add(AbstractButton ab)
  - Here, ab is a reference to the button to be added to the group.

### *Tabbed Panes*

- A tabbed pane is a component that appears as a group of folders in a file cabinet.
- Each folder has a title. When a user selects a folder, its contents become visible. Only one of the folders may be selected at a time.
- Tabbed panes are commonly used for setting configuration options.
- Tabbed panes are encapsulated by the JTabbedPane class, which extends JComponent. We will use its default constructor. Tabs are defined via the following method:
  - void addTab(String str, Component comp)
    - Here, str is the title for the tab, and
    - comp is the component that should be added to the tab.
    - Typically, a JPanel or a subclass of it is added.
- The general procedure to use a tabbed pane in an applet is outlined here:
  - Create a JTabbedPane object.
- Call addTab( ) to add a tab to the pane.
- (The arguments to this method define the title of the tab and the component it contains.)
- Repeat step 2 for each tab.
- Add the tabbed pane to the content pane of the applet.

### *Scroll Panes*

- A scroll pane is a component that presents a rectangular area in which a component may be viewed. Horizontal and/or vertical scroll bars may be provided if necessary.
- Scroll panes are implemented in Swing by the JScrollPane class, which extends JComponent. Some of its constructors are :
  - JScrollPane(Component comp)
  - JScrollPane(int vsb, int hsb)
  - JScrollPane(Component comp, int vsb, int hsb)
    - Here, comp is the component to be added to the scroll pane.
    - vsb and hsb are int constants that define when vertical and horizontal

scroll bars for this scroll pane are shown.

- These constants are defined by the ScrollPaneConstants interface.
- HORIZONTAL_SCROLLBAR_ALWAYS
- .HORIZONTAL_SCROLLBAR_AS_NEEDED
- VERTICAL_SCROLLBAR_ALWAYS
- VERTICAL_SCROLLBAR_AS_NEEDED

- Here are the steps to follow to use a scroll pane in an applet:
    - Create a JComponent object.
    - Create a JScrollPane object.
    - The arguments to the constructor specify thecomponent and the policies for vertical and horizontal scroll bars.
    - Add the scroll pane to the content pane of the applet.

### *Trees*

- Data Model - TreeModel
    - default: DefaultTreeModel
    - getChild, getChildCount, getIndexOfChild, getRoot, isLeaf
- Selection Model - TreeSelectionModel
- View - TreeCellRenderer
    - getTreeCellRendererComponent
- Node – DefaultMutableTreeNode

### *Tables*

- A table is a component that displays rows and columns of data. You can drag the cursor on column boundaries to resize columns. You can also drag a column to a new position.
- Tables are implemented by the JTable class, which extends JComponent.
- One of its constructors is :
    - JTable(Object data[ ][ ], Object colHeads[ ])
        - Here, data is a two-dimensional array of the information to be presented.
        - colHeads is a one-dimensional array with the column headings.
- Here are the steps for using a table in an applet:
    - Create a JTable object.

- Create a JScrollPane object.
- The arguments to the constructor specify the table and the policiesfor vertical and horizontal scroll barsAdd the table to the scroll pane.
- Add the scroll pane to the content pane of the applet